W9-BJN-411

Ladies First, *Please!*

Celebrating first ladies who served with principals and presidents in the Valley 1895-2013

BETTY H. RIVERS

Academic Building
Photo courtesy FVSU Archives

FOREWORD

"It feels like members of the family have assembled for a great reunion"—Betty Jean Hubbard Rivers, in the Afterword to *Ladies First, Please! Celebrating first ladies who served with principals and presidents in the Valley 1895-2013*. When First Lady Betty Rivers experienced the rewards of mounting a museum exhibition about the history of Fort Valley State University, she became inspired to share this story with more people. Thus was *born Ladies First, Please! Celebrating first ladies who served with principals and presidents in the Valley 1895-2013*. This book brings to life all the spouses of Fort Valley State University's principals and presidents, so that we can feel ourselves present during each succeeding administration, at each principal's and president's side. Welcome to the reunion!

Dr. *Anna Holloway*

Dean, Graduate Studies and Extended Education

Ladies First, Please! is the culmination of a dream through efforts of someone who saw a need and did what it took to resolve it. There is a 'legacy' of noble women who were 'the wind behind the men' who have served as principals and presidents of Fort Valley High and Industrial School, Fort Valley Junior College, Fort Valley Normal and Industrial School, Fort Valley State College, and the Fort Valley State University.

All too often, attention is given to great men without alluding to their success enhanced by their silent partners. "Behind every great man is a strong woman." These wives silhouetted their programs and often created their own projects. Yet as the various accomplishments are credited to their husbands, there is no mention of the outstanding, constructive support generated and given by their wives.

First School Bus
Photo courtesy FVSU Archives

Here, at last, is tangible evidence of some of the cohesive work promoted for our institution by these 'First Ladies'. Too much credit cannot be afforded our FVSU First Lady, Mrs. Betty Jean Hubbard Rivers, because she went beyond the call of duty to conduct in-depth research of an issue which had not been done previously.

It is an honor for me to extend an invitation to you to become informed and appreciative.

Wilmetta S. Langston ('57)
Archivist, Hunt Memorial Library

ISBN: 1497534887
ISBN 13: 9781497534889

In Gratitude

The Rivers' Family
Larry Omar, Betty Jean, Larry Eugene and Linje' Eugene
Photo courtesy FVSU Marketing and Communications Office

Table of Contents

Introduction

The history of Fort Valley State University begins in nineteenth century Houston County, Georgia outside the city limits of Fort Valley on Marshallville Road, renamed State University Drive. This section of middle Georgia, well-known for succulent peaches, delectable pecans and bountiful cotton crops saw attempts to provide education for African Americans starting in the Reconstruction era.

Later, in the era of segregation, eighteen black and white men had the courage and foresight to petition the Houston County superior court in 1895 for a charter to start a special school for blacks in Fort Valley. The court granted the petition. On January 6, 1896, with the petition providing the legal basis, the Fort Valley High and Industrial High School (later renamed Fort Valley Normal and Industrial School in 1932) was established.

In 1939, the Board of Regents of the University System of Georgia merged the Teachers and Agricultural College of Forsyth with the Fort Valley Normal and Industrial School making it a four-year institution and renaming it Fort Valley State College.

In 1947, the Board of Regents adopted a resolution moving the land-grant status from Savannah State College to Fort Valley State College thereby designating the school as Georgia's 1890 Land-Grant College for Negroes.

Continuing its recognition of the school's successful development, the Board of Regents granted Fort Valley State 'university' status in 1996 and renamed it Fort Valley State University. During its 118-year history, two principals and eight presidents, along with their first ladies, labored to transform Fort Valley State University into the vibrant, ever-growing and revered institution of higher education it is today. The following individuals provided leadership: John W. Davison, (first principal, Fort Valley High and Industrial School), Henry Alexander Hunt (second principal, Fort Valley High and Industrial School/Fort Valley Normal and Industrial School), Dr. Horace Mann Bond (1st president), Dr. Cornelius Vanderbilt Troup (2nd president), Dr. Waldo William

Emerson Blanchet (3rd president), Dr. Cleveland William Pettigrew (4th president), Dr. Luther Burse (5th president), Dr. Oscar Lewis Prater (6th president), Dr. Kofi Lomotey (7th president) and Dr. Larry Eugene Rivers (8th president). Additionally, three acting presidents served at the institution: Dr. Louis Sullivan, Dr. Melvin Walker and Dr. William Harris.

As noted earlier, Fort Valley State University's history spans well over a century, and a local museum invited Fort Valley State University to tell its intriguing story. In April 2010, The Tubman African American Museum and Fort Valley State University hosted a ribbon cutting ceremony to present a new historical exhibition, *The Transformation of a Growing Institution since 1895 – Fort Valley State University*, April 16 – July 3.

This exhibition explored and celebrated the history and growth of this prestigious institution, The Fort Valley State University. Curated by faculty, Berry Jordan, first lady Betty Rivers, students at Fort Valley State University and members of the Peach County Community, the historical exhibition employed a combination of vintage and contemporary photographs, documents, and historical artifacts. The exhibit revealed the story of the physical growth of the University campus, the development of its liberal arts curriculum, and its expanding, positive impact on the community, the State of Georgia and the nation.

Hundreds of individuals in middle Georgia, many becoming new patrons of the museum, visited the historical exhibit during its debut at the Tubman Museum. In fall 2010, the exhibit relocated to the Fort Valley State University Art Gallery and Studio in downtown Fort Valley. On this occasion, faculty, staff and new students toured the gallery, eager to learn more about Georgia's ninth oldest public institution of higher education.

The excitement generated from audiences about the significance of the historical exhibit elevated it to a new level. The vision of a book appeared on the author's radar screen. An excellent foundation for such a volume had been laid by the extensive research in student yearbooks and bulletins, campus newspapers and photo collections in the Hunt Memorial Library Archives done by those preparing the exhibit. Writing this book offered me the chance to tell intriguing, never before told stories about Fort Valley State University legends in both biographical and pictorial format.

As has been often stated, "Behind every good man is a good woman." Such has been the case with regard to the principals and presidents of Fort Valley State University. The desire to learn more about the spouses of the principals and presidents inspired me to expand this research. Interviews shared by their families and friends yielded much more personal and intriguing tidbits of information about these phenomenal women. So, Hattie Davison, Florence Johnson Hunt, Julia Agnes Washington Bond, Katye Murphy Troup, Josephine Lavizzo Blanchet, Edwina Phinazee Pettigrew, Mamie Balbon Burse, Jacqueline Polson Prater, Aama Nahuja and Betty Hubbard Rivers will share the stage along with their spouses as pioneers who shaped the history of this educational institution. I also extend special recognition to Jeraldine Wooden Walker and Wanda F. Harris who assisted their spouses during their tenure as acting presidents.

Capitalizing on the work of local scholars for this new initiative proved beneficial. For instance, Dr. Donnie D. Bellamy, retired Regents' professor and author of *Light in the Valley*, provided a pictorial history of the Fort Valley State College. Additionally, Bellamy's synopsis of first ladies included as a supplement in the 1999 Founders' Day Program, proved helpful as well. And Dr. Fred van Hartesveldt, Fort Valley State University Professor of History and Head of the History, Geography, Political Science and Criminal Justice Department, authored an essay published in *The Varieties of Women's Experiences, Portraits of Southern Women in the Post-Civil War Century*, which portrayed Florence Johnson Hunt as a significant force during her husband's tenure as the second principal at Fort Valley High and Industrial School. My research effort also included other related sources.

This book is penned with the hope that the biographical sketches will inspire others to honor legends in the Valley. Throughout the course of this project many individuals have offered assistance. Berry Jordan (deceased), my mentor, and walking historian, deserves accolades for inspiring me to move forward and share stories about Fort Valley State University legends. I am grateful for invaluable services rendered by Chata Spikes, Tracey Marshall, Dr. Yvonne Oliver, Dr. Anna Holloway,

Dr. Fred van Hartesveldt, Dr. Julius Scipio, Mayor John Stumbo, Dr. Andy Ambrose, Cheryl Jordan, Bobby Dickey, James Khoury, Barbara Davis, Albert O'Bryant, Laura A. Brown, Jason Groover and Dontay Farley. Families, relatives and friends of the featured legends shared precious photos and timeless information – Dr. Waldo Blanchet, Geri Blanchet, Dr. Luther Burse, Beverly P. Hicks, Dr. Everett Troup, C. V. Troup, III, James George Bond, Dr. Melody Carter, Dr. Ira Hicks, Margaret McCormick, Robert Ross, Shonda Lewis, Edward Boston, Aama Nahuja, Dorothy Crumbly, Victoria Dubriel, Dan Archer and Marquinta Gonzalez.

Odd Fellows Hall
Photo courtesy FVSU Archives

Wilmetta Jackson, FVSU Hunt Memorial Library archivist, assisted with my research by sharing documents preserved in the Heritage Collection. Mr. Frank Mahitab, Director, Hunt Memorial Library, offered consistent encouragement, along with Dr. Annie Payton, former director of the library. Lisa Scipio and Victoria Sturn worked tirelessly to get the manuscript and photos in great shape. My spouse, Dr. Larry E. Rivers, provided support and other resources needed to get this project started through completion. Of course, our sons, Larry O. and Linje' E. always encourage me to move forward with my initiatives. It is with gratitude that I say, thanks to all who helped me write my first book about Valley legends, *Ladies First, Please!*

Academic Building
Photo courtesy FVSU Archives

Chapter 1

First Lady Hattie Davison
Served with John W. Davison, 1895-1903

When Donnie D. Bellamy penned *Light in the Valley*, he started with the great work of John W. Davison, founder, Fort Valley High and Industrial School in 1895. "The vision and wisdom of eighteen black and white men lead to the establishment of a school for blacks, with Davison chosen as principal. He explained that the first work of FVHI was to prepare teachers in the district "for more competent and conscientious service in public school work." Davison felt that this task was necessary before "Practical industrial work for the masses could be done."

According to the manuscript federal census of 1900, Davison was born in September 1862; and he was married to Hattie who was eleven years his junior. Although information about Hattie was not available to this writer, Davison was born in Crawford County, Georgia; and he attended Atlanta University. He dropped out of Atlanta University during his senior year on April 18, 1889, and John and Hattie married the following year. Davison and Hattie were probably the first two teachers of about seventy-five students at the school which came to be known as The Fort Valley High and Industrial School (FVHI).

My research also revealed little about Hattie Davison. As Bellamy noted earlier, she likely assisted with teaching responsibilities. This was necessary because of the lack of sufficient funds for school operations. Bellamy also quoted another source noting that, "the number of students was altogether too great for the teaching force, and for the first two years two teachers were compelled to attempt to give instruction to from 250 to 300 students. Based on the foregoing, it appears that Hattie Davison supported her husband's efforts, against the odds, to provide a quality education for their students. Hattie Davison mentored and advised students about their goals and aspirations. Through her service, students were taught to study and prepare themselves to get jobs and help their families. Of course, great teachers leave a lasting impression on students.

Bellamy also recognized a few distinguished graduates during the Davison's tenure at FVHI. Certainly Hattie beamed with proud when Alberta L. Mack, an honor graduate, was awarded a degree in 1903. Later, Mack's daughter, FVSC alumna, left the institution $380,000 in her will. Hattie also had the pleasure of seeing Austin Thomas graduate from FVHI in 1902. After earning the B.A. and LL.B degrees, he became Georgia's first black judge and was appointed a municipal judge in Atlanta. In conclusion, Hattie Davison played a significant role in getting the school started also.

SOURCE: Donnie D. Bellamy, Light in the Valley: A Pictorial History of Fort Valley State College since 1895 (Virginia Beach, V.: Donning Company, 1996), 14, 25

John W. Davison
First Principal, Fort Valley High and Industrial School
1895-1903
Photo courtesy FVSU Archives

I have always thought that the colored man, when it comes to schools for his own people, should not only have considerable voice, but should be required to largely govern them, for the object of all education is to develop the power of self-government.

John W. Davison

Donnie D. Bellamy, *Light in the Valley: A Pictorial History of Fort Valley State College since 1895* (Virginia Beach, Va.: Donning Company, 1996)

In Donnie Bellamy's book, *Light in the Valley*, his portrayal of John W. Davison, founder, Fort Valley High and Industrial School, intrigued this author. According to Bellamy, "In the beginning there was a school and there was John Wesley Davison, leader of the founders of Fort Valley State College. The school was chartered outside of the city limits of Fort Valley in Houston County on the Marshallville Road (currently State University Drive and formerly South Macon Street) in middle Georgia. Early in October 1895, Davison and several men started planning the school. The meetings were held in the Odd Fellows Lodge Hall on O'Neal Street. Charlie H. Nixon, a member of Usher's Temple Colored Methodist Episcopal (CME) Church, served as secretary of the group "planning . . . for a larger school."

"On November 6, 1895, Bellamy noted, eighteen men, including fifteen blacks and three whites, petitioned the Superior Court of Houston County located in Perry for a charter to legalize the school." According to to the application, the purpose of the institution was:

. . . the furthering, (and) promoting of the cause of mental and manual education in the State of Georgia and the Special purpose is to have, acquire, hold, manage and control grounds, buildings, machinery and outfit for the successful conducting of a school for the higher mental and manual education of the youths and children of Georgia, also to elect teachers and have general control of all matters connected with the carrying out of the said school."

According to the federal census of 1900 in Bellamy's research, "Davison was born in September 1862 in Crawford County, Georgia. He attended Atlanta University (now Clark Atlanta University). But, Davison dropped out of college during his senior year on April 18, 1889, and married Hattie the following year. It's highly possible that Davison and Hattie were the first two teachers of about seventy-five students at the school that later came to be known as the Fort Valley High and Industrial School (FVHI).

The original Board of Trustees selected Davison as principal and appointed him for life in October 1895. The first work of FVHI was to prepare the teachers in the district "for more competent and conscientious service in public school work." Davison felt that this work was necessary before "practical industrial work for the masses could be done."

Bellamy explained, "Throughout Davison's years as principal, the school lacked sufficient funds to operate or provide high quality work. The school was run largely off solicited contributions, which were generally small. As early as March 1896, the Board of Trustees was forced to rent out a room of the first school building on the new campus. According to one source, "The first structure was a two-story wooden building which was placed on the spot where St. Luke's Episcopal Church later stood." "During his tenure, Davison devoted more attention to the ideal of industrial training than he was given credit. Writing to George Foster Peabody of the General Education Board, Davison noted "it has been our desire, from the beginning, to make this an industrial school after the order of Hampton and Tuskegee." "The school did not have a strong industrial program under Davison's leadership, however, because of insufficient funds; essential equipment for that kind of training was quite expensive. Nonetheless, local whites did withhold their support, because of what they thought was the school's curriculum under Davison." "School treasurer Gray wrote in 1902, "I think the watchword should be, more work, less Latin, less Greek." The available records, however, suggest that Latin was not taught at the institution before the 1920s and Greek probably ever. Gray seems to have been exaggerating his opposition to an academic curriculum for African Americans rather than describing the actual situation."

Bellamy shared also, "Davison's philosophy of blacks' control of their educational institutions also caused some local whites concern. Commenting on his philosophy of education for blacks, Davison wrote to a white philanthropist in 1902: "I have always thought that the colored man, when it comes to schools for his own people, should not only have considerable voice, but should be required to largely govern them, for the object of all education is to develop the power of self-government." "A very influential white Northerner who was in frequent contact with Fort Valley's white leadership, said of Davison, "I don't like him. He has a furtive glance that is far from assuring...."

Under his helm, Anna T. Jeanes, Bellamy mentioned, "The Philadelphia Quakeress and the financier of the well-known Jeanes Fund made a contribution. She did this before the Fund was established in 1907. Jeanes donated $5,000 to construct a dormitory for girls, named in her honor. In the years before, the General Education Board made its first grant of $1,000, but Jeanes' donation was the largest awarded to an institution for blacks in Georgia."

Also under Davison's helm noted Bellamy, "Austin Thomas Walden, later one of the South's most prominent lawyers and Georgia's first black judge, completed his academic work at FVHI in 1902. He earned the B.A. degree at Atlanta University in 1907 and the LL.B. degree at the University of Michigan in 1911. In 1963, he became Georgia's first black judge when he was appointed a municipal judge in Atlanta, a city that owed much to Walden, the son of ex-slaves and sharecroppers. He was one of FVHI's distinguished graduates and one of Georgia's most prominent lawyers. Alberta I. Mack, an honor graduate in 1903, also should be credited to Davison's regime. She was the mother of Ruth Peyton, the alumna who left the institution a $380,000 bequest. Most of all, Davison got the school started and operated it against many odds."

In summary, Donnie D. Bellamy portrays John W. Davison as a man before his time. Through his noble efforts in the late 1890s and early 1900s, Davison paved the way that led to the establishment of middle Georgia's premiere institution of higher education for blacks. Oftentimes the lack of financial resources hindered progress, but Davison's vision and determination to educate rural Georgians persevered.

Historical Timeline: John W. Davison, 1895-1903

1895   The Fort Valley High and Industrial School (FVHI) founded
        by leading Negro and White citizens

        John W. Davison led chartering and was selected as first principal
        at FVHI.

1896   First school building constructed on new campus

1902   William Merida Hubbard (Negro) and five White citizens of
        Forsyth petitioned the Superior Court of Monroe County for a
        charter to incorporate a new school for Negroes; the charter was
        granted under the name Forsyth Industrial School.

1903   Forsyth Industrial School renamed Forsyth Normal and
        Industrial School.

        Anna T. Jeanes, philanthropist, donated $5,000 for erection of
        girls' dorm.

        John W. Davison resigned as principal at Fort Valley High and
        Industrial School. Gabriel Bonaparte Miller, FVHI carpentry
        instructor, appointed as acting principal (1903-1904)

SOURCES: Donnie D. Bellamy, *Light in the Valley: A Pictorial History of Fort
Valley State College since 1895* (Virginia Beach, Va.: Donning Company, 1996),
11, 14, 16, 17, 25; http://www.fvsu.edu /about/history.

Academic Building
Photo courtesy FVSU Archives

Florence J. Hunt
Photo courtesy FVSU Archives

Henry and Florence Hunt
Photo courtesy FVSU Archives

Chapter 2

First Lady Florence Johnson Hunt
Served with Henry Alexander Hunt, 1904-1938

Christmas! A mere sounding of the word and we are flooded with a rush of happy thoughts and memories. The faces of children on Christmas morning, the ecstasies of delight at discovery after discovery, the joyous relief after seemingly endless days of delicious expectancy—the happiness of giving, the sights and sounds and tastes and odors—Christmas tide is surely the part of the year which is epitomized in the word "delight." And yet not a stone's throw from our library door, there are children tonight who have never known the real thrill and joy of the Christmas spirit, who have never awakened to rush pell-mell into a tree bedecked room with its lights and its tinsel, to find spread out for their delight, the treasures of childhood. Within the shadow of our buildings are homes that on Christmas Eve will be fortunate to have food for growing little stomachs and fire to warm little ragged bodies. There shall be for them no thrill of joy on Christmas morning; they shall acclaim the advent of the Christ Child with dull eyes and a strange yearning. We hope not to darken for the shadow of a moment the unalloyed happiness of any one's Christmas by turning their thoughts into such a home, but if you could know the torrent of sheer joyousness you would release by your response to our Christmas appeal, it would give added pleasure to your already bounteous store. You would give joy where there is now sorrow; you would give light where darkness now chills little souls.

Florence Johnson Hunt

The Fort Valley Message, Christmas, Vol. II, December 1929, No. 16

I believe when one has done his or her best he feels it deep down within his soul and he has a satisfaction and joy that he otherwise could not have.

Florence J. Hunt

The Fort Valley Message, Vol. XIII, No. 4, Fort Valley, Georgia, June 1939

Florence Johnson Hunt
Photo courtesy FVSU Archives

By 1830, slavery had become a significant part of North Carolina and other southern states, but great jubilation came when it ended in 1865. One year later, in the fall of 1866, Columbus and Eliza Johnson, former slaves, welcomed the birth of a baby girl, Florence, born in Raleigh. This little bundle of joy made her parents happy, coming after two sons. Eventually, five more siblings joined the family. Mr. Johnson worked as a day laborer, and Mrs. Johnson used her culinary and laundry skills to earn much needed money to help support the family also.

The Johnsons encouraged their children to get a good education and made provisions to ensure success. Influenced by big brother, Edward, who entered Atlanta University by 1878 and earned an undergraduate degree four years later, Florence followed the same path. In 1889, her parents celebrated another Atlanta University graduate when she earned a bachelor's degree in education. She returned to North Carolina and entered the teaching profession.

While at Atlanta University, she met a handsome, religious, bright, young man who would later find employment in Charlotte, North

Carolina. In the fall of 1891, Henry Alexander Hunt joined the faculty of Biddle University (now Johnson C. Smith) as superintendent of the Industrial Department. Biddle's new president, D. J. Sanders, hired Hunt, the institution's first black faculty member.

In late spring on June 14, 1893, Florence Johnson and Henry Hunt exchanged wedding vows in Raleigh. The Hunts started their family with Dorothy and later had a second daughter Adele, followed by a son Hal.

Mr. and Mrs. Hunt worked together in harmony, as a couple. She contributed to the family's income by offering boarding to Biddle University

  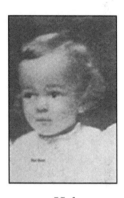

Dorothy	Adele	Hal
Photo courtesy	Photo courtesy	Photo courtesy
FVSU Archives	FVSU Archives	FVSU Archives

personnel in their home. On many occasions, Mr. Hunt sought his wife's advice, including his plan to host the first black farmers' conference in North Carolina.

Mrs. Hunt joined several professional organizations such as the North Carolina Women's Christian Temperance Union (WCTU). However, in 1889, the African American women in North Carolina separated from the predominately white state organization. From that point, the nation's only black women's temperance group operated under the umbrella of the national organization.

The WCTU sponsored a variety of projects that included hosting educational campaigns, holding temperance rallies and petitioning Congress to ban the trade of alcohol. Additionally, the WCTU ministered to prisoners and narcotics abusers. Mrs. Hunt edited the organization's state journal. She was also a proud member of the National Association of Colored Women and worked diligently to support the organization.

Life was good for the Hunts in Raleigh, but an opportunity of a lifetime changed their path. The Fort Valley High and Industrial School (FVHI) trustees urged Mr. Hunt to succeed John W. Davison and become the second principal of the school. After he accepted the offer, the family packed belongings and moved to Georgia in 1904.

As author Fred van Hartesveldt reveals in his essay, "Florence Johnson Hunt 1866-1953—Days of Labor of an African American Woman," Mrs. Hunt vividly described her first impression of Fort Valley:

> The old gray horse and the buggy waiting at the station. The lifting of two small girls and a boy from the buggy to be 'toted' down in the arms of stronger boys. The water standing around the old house. The rooms, so large, so empty and bare. The old log barn. The old laundry stood right alongside the principal's house, Anna T. Jeanes Hall dormitory partially completed. The three-room school building across the road. The deep cellar surrounded by a three-foot brick wall and filled with water. The beginning of another building. The school grounds, a sand bed, millions, billions, trillions of pebbles, but trees, shrubbery, lawns—where, oh where, were they!
>
> The big pond between the school and Central of Georgia Railway so near. Men, women, children paddling in the water, riding in bateaux, shooting the bullfrogs. At night the croak of the frogs, the yell of drinkers, gamblers on the railroad banks, green slimy puddles of water, mosquitoes, malaria, and typhoid.

Mrs. Hunt observed the scarcity of gardens, poor nutrition, and the absence of public health, no colored doctors, and two-month school terms because youth labor was needed. These issues and related matters helped shape what would become her social outreach campaign.

Another priority of the Hunts focused on the financial solvency of the struggling school. She traveled north with her husband, and sometimes alone, to meet new friends and raise money in support of the institution's operations and physical plant. This initiative generated much needed money from well-heeled individuals including Royal C. Peabody, Julius Rosenwald, John D. Rockefeller, Andrew Carnegie, Collis P. Huntington and Anna T. Jeanes. As a result of their initiatives, the campus experienced widespread construction of new buildings and support for educational programs.

Mrs. Hunt assisted in other ways as a teacher of English, stenography and literature, and as director of girls' industries (Huntington and Jeanes Halls, Infirmary, Laundry). She served as Assistant Principal during her husband's absence from the school on official business and as a member of the governing board.

The Hunts' efforts generated local, regional and national appeal. Their great work did not go unnoticed by community leaders and residents. They engaged in many community initiatives that benefited the school and community such as Sunday schools, Thanksgiving rallies and May Day celebrations.

Mrs. Hunt served as a crucial link between the school and community. Her efforts gained funds to erect an infirmary to replace the school's old Health Center. The infirmary served both FVHI and the community, black and white residents. She established the Gano Parent-Teacher Association that allowed parents to have a voice in local education. The annual Christmas tree party, hosted by Mrs. Hunt, lifted the spirits of children and the less fortunate who received gifts to celebrate the Yuletide season.

A compassionate and caring individual, Mrs. Hunt worked with northern Quaker families to house pregnant black girls who lacked family support in Georgia. Additionally, she raised funds that were specifically earmarked for their educational and vocational training.

Mrs. Hunt became affiliated with the Georgia Federation of Colored Women's Clubs that focused on youth and education. This initiative led to another fundraising effort for the construction of a school to train delinquent young women. Her work as social reformer garnered accolades from Mary McLeod Bethune who declared, "She was a courageous woman and a determined spirit, and yet her deep humility attracted all to follow her with faith and devotion."

In 1931, she was elected the ninth president of the Georgia Federation of Colored Women's Clubs. Under her leadership, the Federation launched a successful campaign to get a training school for delinquent black girls in Georgia. The Training School of Delinquent Colored Girls opened November 1943, in Macon, Georgia. This facility provided a refuge for girls who were incarcerated and made to perform menial tasks without any hope for rehabilitation.

Florence Johnson Hunt made significant contributions as a pioneer and social reformer. She and her husband transformed Fort Valley High and Industrial School, later renamed Fort Valley Normal and Industrial School, into a thriving and progressive institution of higher education. Mrs. Hunt deserved far more credit for her work than she received during her lifetime. By all accounts, Mrs. Florence Johnson Hunt will be remembered as a phenomenal woman who greatly enhanced the enormous contributions of her husband to the school.

SOURCE: "Florence Johnson Hunt 1866-1953 Days of Labor of an African American Woman," essay by Fred van Hartesveldt in *The Varieties of Women's Experiences Portrait of Southern Women in the Post-Civil War Century*, edited by Larry Eugene Rivers and Canter Brown, Jr., Gainesville: University Press of Florida, 2009, 172-178; 180-183

Henry Alexander Hunt, Jr.
Second Principal, Fort Valley High
And Industrial School, 1904-1938
Photo courtesy FVSU Archives

It was through Dr. Peabody (George Foster Peabody) more than any other individual that Mrs. Hunt and I were influenced to leave a circle of congenial companions and friends, a comfortable home and a good position in North Carolina to undertake the building up of an institution to serve a sadly underprivileged group in the Black Belt section of Georgia. Immediately upon our arrival, Dr. Peabody showed his deep understanding by making a contribution to be used at the Principal's discretion for things which would be needed in such a situation and yet which might not easily be explained in a budget. This generous act was characteristic of the man and was continued in one-way and another until the end.

Henry A. Hunt

The Fort Valley Message, June 1938, Vol. XI, No 4, "George Foster Peabody – World Citizen and Lover of Men."

For more than fifty years I knew Henry Hunt: in boyhood as a fair player, a hard player; later, as a sympathetic man, with a keen sense of humor; a persistent worker and a man of action with a philosophy of life, but no philosopher, no dreamer to rest satisfied with his dream, a man who reveled in execution, and looked at failure only a new beginning; who wrought before he taught, because he thought example availed more than precept; who had sympathy for the evil doer but no toleration of the evil deed; who thought we should seek to know people; who believed in people even to his hurt, and especially in the possibilities of the humblest and poorest urchins with whom he dealt; who believed that friendship meant serving rather than using friends; who had a passion for cooperation and who, if he left a few unfulfilled hopes that burdened his heart, we are sure one of them was that his group would grow more and more into self-dependence through greater and greater cooperation. That is the sort of rare leader Negro education and the Nation has lost in Henry A. Hunt.

The Fort Valley Normal and Industrial School is his monument by his own hands. He left it unencumbered, with money to pay all of its debts, and holding the highest rank among junior colleges of the South. He has set a high standard of accomplishment for whoever follows him in his work.

George A. Towns

The Fort Valley Message, Vol. XII, December 1938, No. 2

This amazing account of Henry Alexander Hunt is based on the research found in Dr. Donnie Bellamy's book, Light in the Valley." According to Bellamy, "Henry was the fifth of eight racially mixed children. His family resided in Hancock County, Georgia. His mother, Mariah, had some of the fundamentals of an education, and she had studied music. Mariah's "husband," one writer held, "was not a cultured man of letters, but he [Henry Alexander Hunt, Sr.] was a successful farmer and tanner . . . who managed a good business and fulfilled his civic responsibilities." Although available evidence suggests that the couple shared the same household before the Civil War, they maintained separate households after the war. Henry recalled in July 1930 that he and his brothers and sisters attended "the little unpainted schoolhouse that was open for three months each year. There, on those crude benches, they caught in some miraculous way the desire for book learning and the determination to get it." After he completed the formal education available to him in Hancock County, Henry, at sixteen, followed his older sister Adella and enrolled at Atlanta University."

"As a student at Atlanta University, noted Bellamy, Hunt demonstrated his qualities as a leader among his fellow students. George A. Towns, a college classmate and longtime friend, observed that "Hunt was the most popular of his class as evidenced by the choice of him for captain of the baseball team, as judge in the moot court and as president of the Phi Kappa Society." Continuing, Towns also described Hunt as "active, agile, and alert. In study, at work, at play, he moved swiftly and effectively, and his actions were not spasmodic, but they were directed by thoughts, which gave reason for what he did." Hunt had a deep interest in the industrial education program. He and two of his classmates, according to one witness, "were the best workmen in the shop," but Hunt "would turn out work more rapidly than the others, and it would be very well done." "In addition to his college course, Hunt learned the builder's trade." During his vacations, he worked as a journeyman carpenter to earn money for his education." He helped with the construction of the state capitol and schoolhouses in Alabama and Georgia.

In 1890, Hunt earned the Bachelor of Arts degree from Atlanta University. He went out to open up the field of education for blacks. His first job after college was as a teacher in Jackson, Georgia; but in less than a year Hunt moved to Charlotte, North Carolina to be the new principal of the main public grammar school for Negroes. Once again in less than a year, Hunt attracted the attention of a new potential employer. At the behest of President D. J. Sanders of Biddle (now Johnson C. Smith) University, in November 1891, Hunt became a university professor.

Based on Bellamy's research, "During the period of thirteen and one-half years at Johnson C. Smith, Hunt served as superintendent of the Industrial Department and proctor over the boys. The boys "idolized him because of his virile mind and youthful spirit." His influence over the boys was so great that they began to take more pride in their personal appearance, and they were moved to acquire additional clothes to supplement their gifts of Northern charity."

On June 14, 1893 in Raleigh, NC, Hunt married Florence S. Johnson, his college sweetheart and sister of Edward A. Johnson, who was the first black assemblyman of New York. A Raleigh, North Carolina native, Florence was a student in the Normal Department of Atlanta University when Henry was pursuing his college work. During their marriage, the couple had three children—Dorothy, Adele and Hal. After Henry's appointment as FVHI's principal in 1902, Hunt labored, with extreme sacrifice and unstinted devotion, side by side with her husband. Among the many duties that she assumed as wife of the principal, Florence taught English, stenography and literature, served as director of girls' industries (Huntington and Jeanes Halls, Infirmary, Laundry), and a member of the Governing Board. *The Fort Valley Message*, published quarterly by the Fort Valley Normal and Industrial School, listed Florence as Associate Editor. During her husband's absence from the school on official business, she served as Assistant Principal. As a social reformer, Florence became a spokeswoman for the anti-lynching movement. In 1931, she was elected the ninth president of the Georgia Federation of Colored Women's Clubs. Under her leadership, the Federation launched a successful campaign to get a training school for delinquent black girls in Georgia. After hosting various funding raising campaigns and securing a substantial grant from the federal government, the school was constructed in Macon and opened in 1943. Of course, this only provides a glimpse of Florence's activities during their long tenure at the school.

As Bellamy indicated earlier, "Hunt returned to his native Georgia to provide leadership for a black rural educational awakening. Towards the end of 1903, Wallace Buttrick and George Foster Peabody of the General

Education Board (GEB) had started negotiating with him "to give up his work at Biddle University and go into the Black Belt of Georgia for the purpose of building up an institution of the Hampton-Tuskegee type for Negroes in the section." Hunt's decision to return to Georgia "was urgently re-enforced" by one of his sisters, Adella Hunt Logan, one of the pioneer teachers of Tuskegee Institute and the wife of Warren Logan, the treasurer of Mr. Booker T. Washington's school. The Hunts were "influenced to leave a circle of congenial companions and friends, a comfortable home and a good position . . . to undertake the building up of an institution to serve a sadly underprivileged group in the Black Belt section of Georgia." They "decided that the call was one of real service and agreed to accept." The FVHI's board of trustees hired Henry A. Hunt in 1904, as the second principal to help the school get back onto a solid, financial footing."

Bellamy also stated, "Hunt envisioned a grand expansion of FVHI and chose to model it after Alabama's Tuskegee Institute founded by notable African-American leader Booker T. Washington. He introduced trade courses into the school's curriculum to attract additional students after diligent efforts to raise funds from philanthropists. The idea worked. Enrollment increased from 1904 to 1938. In 1908, Hunt obtained $25,000 from the estate of Collis P. Huntington, a great railroad financier, for the construction of Huntington Hall, a girls' dormitory. To ensure the institution's financial stability, FVHI affiliated itself with the American Church Institute for Negroes for the Protestant Episcopal Church in 1919. The church's backing financed the construction of Ohio Hall, mentioned previously. Additional monies awarded by the Carnegie Foundation in 1925 erected Carnegie Library. Royal C. Peabody provided the funds for the Peabody Trades Building."

Based on Bellamy's research, "FVHI continued expanding its curriculum throughout the 1920s. A post-high school, baccalaureate year, and later, a teacher's training program were in place by 1927. Liberal arts courses were also added for students. These additions resulted in the designation of FVHI as a Junior College the following year.

At the time of his death the school had thirteen well-designed modern building, a campus with shrubbery and lawns. In spite of perennial financial difficulties, the school had also continued to grow in enrollment and recognition under Hunt's guidance. The enrollment increased from 145 students in 1904 to about 1,000 in 1938, including 103 junior college students. To reflect the growth and expansion of programs, including junior college status, thus, the name was changed to the Fort Valley Normal and Industrial School in 1932. Henry A. Hunt's long tenure of service ceased upon his death on October 1, 1938, in Washington, D. C. Negotiations that commenced before his death to transfer FVNIS to state control and operation were finalized July 1, 1939. Thus, the State Teachers and Agricultural College at Forsyth was consolidated with FVNIS, to form Fort Valley State College."

As articulated by Dr. Donnie D. Bellamy above, whose research on the life of Henry A. Hunt is a major contribution to African American history, Hunt became a dominant fixture in rural middle Georgia from 1904 to 1939. His exceptional leadership advanced Fort Valley High and Industrial School (later changed to Fort Valley High and Normal School) so that it became an institution that offered numerous liberal arts courses. Not only did it advance to the junior college level, but also laid the foundation to become a four-year college in the University of Georgia System. The vision of Henry and Florence to promote the school also resulted in support from philanthropists near and far. Their service to the community had a far-reaching impact on the lives of residents, black and white. Indeed, Henry Alexander Hunt became an indispensable man in education and politics in middle Georgia during the 1920s and 1930s.

Historical Timeline: Henry Alexander Hunt, 1904-1938

1904   Henry Alexander Hunt appointed as second principal, Fort Valley High and Industrial School

1905   Chapel Hall constructed providing classrooms, offices and boys' dormitory rooms; the first library on campus occupied a single room in the facility

1907   Widow of Collis Potter Huntington, railroad financier, contributed $25,000 for a girls' dormitory, Huntington Hall; the building was named in his honor.

1913   FVHI started the first summer school program for Negro teachers in the state of Georgia.

1916   General Education Board provided funds to remodel Jeanes Hall, women's dormitory.

Royal C. Peabody provided funds for construction of the Trades Building that bears his name.

Otis O'Neal hosted the first Ham show with 39 hams and 17 dozen eggs; the show later acquired national fame as the "Ham and Egg Show."

1919   FVHI partnered with the American Church Institute of the Protestant Episcopal Church, a financial supporter.

College laundry erected

1922   Georgia General Assembly passed legislation to make Forsyth Normal and Industrial School the "School for Agriculture and Mechanic Arts for training Negroes" in GA

1925   The Carnegie Foundation provided funds for erection of the Carnegie Library at FVHI.

1926   Trades Building erected and named for Royal C. Peabody, philanthropist

        The first modern barn constructed on the FVHI school farm

1927   Peach County Training School erected with funds provided by the Julius Rosenwald Foundation

1928   FVHI gained junior college status.

1929   Academic Building erected with funds provided by the General Education Board and friends

        Forsyth Normal and Industrial School acquired junior college status.

1930   Ohio Hall, men's dormitory, erected with funds provided by the Episcopal Church of the State of Ohio, the American Church Institute and the General Education Board

        Henry Alexander Hunt awarded the prestigious Spingarn Medal by the NAACP for devoted service to the education of Blacks in rural Georgia

1931   Forsyth Normal and Industrial School renamed "State Teachers and Agriculture College" and included as a unit of the University System of Georgia

Hunt received the William E. Harman Foundation Award for Education and gold medal for distinguished achievement among Negroes.

Hunt was granted a Rosenwald Fellowship for the study of cooperatives in the Scandinavian countries.

1932　Samuel Henry Bishop, philanthropist, donated funds for erection of a dining hall; later named in his honor.

Fort Valley High and Industrial School renamed Fort Valley Normal and Industrial School (FVNIS)

1933　FVNIS Trustees allowed Hunt to serve the Government as Special Assistant to the Governor of the Farm Credit Administration; played useful role by informing Negroes how to gain access to resources of the Farm Credit Administration. Florence Hunt ran the school during her husband's absence.

1934　College infirmary erected and dedicated to Florence Hunt, wife of Henry Alexander Hunt

1937　Robert W. Patton, D.D., Director of the American Church Institute for Negroes, donated funds for erection of the Home Economics Building, named in his honor.

Inaugural publication of *The Fort Valley Message* quarterly newsletter by FVNIS, Henry A. Hunt, editor; George A. Towns and Florence J. Hunt, associate editors

1938　WMAZ Broadcasting Station invited the school's choir to give a series of broadcasts for six Sunday afternoons that consisted mostly of Negro spirituals. These live performances were held on campus before a large audience that included town's people.

Henry Alexander Hunt died October 1, 1938.

SOURCES: Donnie D. Bellamy, *Light in the Valley: A Pictorial History of Fort Valley State College since 1895* (Virginia Beach, Va.: Donning Company, 1996), 28, 29, 30, 48; http://www.fvsu.edu /about/history; The Fort Valley Message, Vol. XII December, 1938, No.2, 1-2

Academic Building
Photo courtesy FVSU Archives

Julia Agnes W. Bond
Photo courtesy James George Bond

Horace and Julia Bond
Photo courtesy James George Bond

Chapter 3

First Lady Julia Agnes Washington Bond
Served with Dr. Horace Mann Bond, 1939 – 1945

He (Horace Mann Bond) wrote in the middle 1930s, and his work was informed by his own life and training as a scholar. Viewed from today's vantage, it may suffer, but the themes from Star Creek resonate today in calls for land and restitution for the victims of racism past, present, and enduring, concern about the critiques of the stability of the black family and lynching-by rural Louisiana mobs then and by more respectable rabble today. I am proud that my mother is given due credit for her part in the project. Given her modest nature, what pleases her is that, twenty-five years after his death (1972), this work will confirm her partner's place in the pantheon of intellectuals of the 1930s and 1940s who helped pioneer the modern interpretation of the southern black family after slavery and Reconstruction.

Julian Bond
The Star Creek Papers, Horace Mann Bond and Julia W. Bond, edited by Adam Fairclough, 1977, the University of Georgia Press, VIII.

Julia Agnes Washington Bond was born on June 20, 1908, in Nashville, Tennessee. Her parents, Daisy Agnes Turner Washington, a teacher, and George Elihu Washington, principal of Pearl High School, were graduates of Fisk University. Mrs. Bond's parents stressed the importance of getting an education and she adhered to their guidance. She attended Meigs Middle Magnet School until the eighth grade and later graduated from Pearl High School at the tender age of sixteen. Like her parents, Mrs. Bond attended Fisk University, earning a B.A. degree in English in 1929. During her senior year, she met a young instructor, Horace Mann Bond, one of the few African American teachers at Fisk University. They entered graduate school at the University of Chicago and married in 1929. She decided to put her graduate studies on hold while her husband pursued his Ph.D. degree at the University of Chicago. They were the parents of three children: Jane Marguerite, Horace Julian and James George.

Dr. Bond's career in academia required the family to relocate to various cities around the nation. He continued his graduate studies, but it would take him twelve years to complete the Ph.D. degree due to immediate family and professional responsibilities.

In 1934, Mrs. Bond and her husband lived in Washington Parish, in rural southeastern Louisiana. While on assignment, Horace Mann Bond conducted a study of rural black schools. His journal provided details about the lives of poor, black farm families. Sixty-three years later, Mrs. Bond would publish *The Star Creek Papers,* a journal detailing the lives of these families among whom she and her husband lived in 1934.

In 1939, the State Teachers and Agriculture College of Forsyth and Fort Valley Normal and Industrial School merged to form Fort Valley State College. In the same year, the Board of Regents offered Bond the presidency at the college. Bond initially consented to serve as acting president for a year and then agreed to be the first official president of Fort Valley State College.

During the summer of 1939, Mrs. Bond and her husband arrived in Fort Valley with Jane, their two year old toddler and first born. The Bonds settled into the president's house. Henry A. Hunt, second principal of Fort Valley Normal and Industrial School, and his family previously occupied this residence. There must have been much excitement and anxiety for Dr. Horace Mann Bond being at the helm of a new state supported school for Negroes, located in the heart of middle Georgia. Before his death in 1938, Hunt appealed to the Board of Regents to take the Fort Valley Normal and Industrial School under its auspices. Using a gift from the Julius Rosenwald Fund, the Georgia Board of Regents acquired the Fort Valley School in June 1939, and made it a four-year unit of the University System. The name of the new senior college was changed to Fort Valley State College. New students arrived in September eager to begin their college experience with the first president of Fort Valley State College and First Lady Julia Agnes Washington Bond.

As first lady, Mrs. Bond's schedule included many traditional events hosted on campus. The college invited special guests to commemorate Hubbard Day, Folk Festival, Ham and Egg Show, Founders Day and seasonal performances sponsored by the College Choir. Of course, she ensured guests were extended warm greetings and entertained during these events.

About six months after their arrival, the Bond's welcomed Julian, their first son, to the family on January 14, 1940. Being a young mother of two children, along with the responsibilities of wife and first lady, Mrs. Bond did not experience any dull moments daily. Of interest, though, is an excerpt from an article written by Megan Rubiner and Candace LaBalle:

> As a native of the South, Julia was used to racial disparity, but she was unwilling to give birth in the primitive hospitals of the highly segregated rural Georgia. To avoid this, she traveled all the way to Nashville, Tennessee, to have her child. Two decades later this son, Julian Bond, became a major force in the fight to end the same segregation that sent his mother to Nashville.

During the same year, students arrived to start the fall quarter. Margaret Wilson left family and many friends to start a new chapter in her life at Fort Valley State College. She became very active as a student and performed with the College Choir, participated in other extracurricular activities, completed college requirements, and donned a cap and gown at the Baccalaureate and Commencement services, along with other proud members of the graduating class of 1944. Fast forward sixty-four years later, Mrs. Margaret Wilson McCormick offered reflections about First Lady Julia Agnes Washington Bond and campus life at FVSC. She recalled, "Mrs. Bond worked at a children's nursery, located within walking distance of her home. The nursery at that time served families of college administrators and professors. Jane and Julian went along with their mother."

Mrs. McCormick expressed her delight when she saw the first lady around campus. As previously noted, Mrs. Bond attended traditional events that required student attendance. Of course, the College Family experienced great jubilation when President Bond conferred degrees to twenty-one students in the first four-year graduating class, June 1941. Summer school Commencement added two.

"Most campus events were held in the auditorium located in Founders Hall," according to Mrs. McCormick. First Lady Bond not only accompanied her husband at traditional events but on other occasions as well. The coronation for the crowning of Miss Rosa Pitts, first campus queen, created excitement around the campus. This special event, among other activities, occurred during Homecoming week, a festive time enjoyed by the college and community.

Mrs. McCormick also mentioned, "The student handbook imposed mandatory attendance at other special programs offered on campus." Students dressed appropriately and enjoyed the Lyceum Series that featured guest artists, special choral performances sponsored by the Music Department during Easter, Christmas and Thanksgiving and plays hosted by the Players Guild each quarter. Dr. and Mrs. Bond attended these events also. Mrs. McCormick commented, "Students, administrators, and faculty anticipated dining together at the annual Thanksgiving dinner, before the holiday break."

Mrs. McCormick marveled about First Lady Bond's presence in the community. The Bond family attended St. Luke's Episcopal Church, which was within walking distance from their residence. First Lady Bond was also a member of Beta Omicron Sigma Graduate Chapter of Delta Sigma Theta Sorority, Inc. As a service sorority, this organization hosted cultural and educational activities in the community. The sorority's undergraduate chapter sponsored activities on campus and around the community; the annual Mother's Day program was a favorite. For ladies night out, "Mrs. Bond and her bridge group spent quality time together," according to Mrs. McCormick.

Julia (front row, far right) with sorority sisters,
Delta Sigma Theta Sorority, Inc.
Photo courtesy FVSU Archives

She explained that after church on Sunday, "The college and community also looked forward to other activities that educated and inspired everyone. The weekly radio broadcast brought students and the campus family together for an hour of exciting programs." The June 1943 issue of the *Peachite* reported, "During the past year, thousands of people throughout central Georgia turned their radio dials to Station WMAZ at 5 o'clock each Sunday afternoon and listened to regular broadcasts from the Fort Valley State College. One of the few colleges in the country to conduct a regular weekly broadcast, The Fort Valley State College established a reputation for presenting varied programs of wide interest and great educational value." McCormick noted, "Sunday evenings were also designated for Vesper, a religious service that required attendance for all college students."

At the end of the year, Dr. and Mrs. Bond hosted a special event at their home. Faculty and friends responded to the invitation and spent an enjoyable evening with the president and first lady, celebrating the start of a new year.

Again in 1944, Mrs. Bond and her husband announced the birth of their third child and second son, James George. She became a busy mother of three; but Mrs. McCormick commented, "hired help enabled Mrs. Bond to manage her schedule more easily."

The Bond Family
Photo courtesy James George Bond

In 1945, First Lady Bond and her family moved to Pennsylvania when Dr. Bond resigned his position at Fort Valley State and accepted the presidency of his alma mater, Lincoln University.

Overall, Margaret McCormick noted, "Mrs. Bond remained a beautiful, quiet, compassionate, friendly, caring, intelligent woman, and a person strongly admired by students and the community alike." Based on the foregoing, Mrs. Julia Agnes Washington Bond led by example and paved the way for others to follow, including the authoress.

On a final note, Mrs. Bond returned to college in 1964 and received a degree later in library science from Atlanta University at the age of fifty-six. She worked for seven years at Atlanta University's Trevor Arnett

Library and retired as a part-time reference librarian at the university's Robert W. Woodruff Library in 2000 at age ninety-two. Dr. Horace Mann Bond died December 21, 1972, at age sixty-eight, and Mrs. Julia Agnes Washington Bond died at ninety-nine years old on November 2, 2007.

SOURCES: The History Makers® Video Oral History Interview with Julia Bond, October 14, 2006, The History Makers®African American Video Oral History Collection, 1900 S. Michigan Avenue, Chicago, Illinois, *Peachite*, 1943-44 and Rubiner, Megan; LaBalle, Candace. "*Bond Julian 1940-.*" Contemporary Black Biography. 2003.

Dr. Horace Mann Bond
First President, Fort Valley State College, 1939-1945
Photo courtesy FVSU Archives

To the first president of The Fort Valley State College, Dr. Horace Mann Bond, we, of the staff, respectfully dedicate the first issue of The Peachite. In making this dedication, it is our fervent hope that the varied accomplishments of this youthful scholar and progressive administrator, will serve as an inspiration to the graduates of the past and to the future graduates of this institution.

The Peachite, Vol. 1, June 1943, No. 1, Dedication, Horace Mann Bond, President of FVSC

"The Fort Valley Ham and Egg Show has become a notable event in American agriculture. Held every year since 1916 in the auditorium of Fort Valley State College, this enterprise reflects the hard work, ingenuity, and imagination of one man. The man is Otis Samuel O'Neal; the movement which has made his work possible, and which he typifies in so many ways, is the Agricultural Extension Service. O'Neal is a Negro county agent working through the Service with Negro farmers. What O'Neal has done for Negro farmers of middle Georgia is a dramatic chapter in the history of the Extension Service."

Dr. Horace Mann Bond

Georgia Agricultural Extension Service, Bulletin 513 – June, 1944 –*Ham and Eggs: A History of the Fort Valley Ham and Egg Show* by H. M. Bond, President, Fort Valley State College

During the six years, from 1939 to 1945, when Dr. Horace Mann Bond was president of the Fort Valley State College, he was considered a friend of the people. Nationally known as a scholar, leader, educator and gentlemen, he nevertheless concentrated his energies toward the advancement of the Negro people of Georgia.

Willie Boyd McNeil

The Peachite, Founders Day Celebration, Volume IV, Number 1, October 1945

James and Jane Brown Bond gave birth to Horace Mann Bond on November 8, 1904, in Nashville, Tennessee. He was the fifth of six children nurtured by his parents. Mrs. Bond received a degree from Oberlin College, and her husband, a minister, earned degrees from Berea College and Oberlin Seminary. James Bond's work history included positions as financial agent for Lincoln Institute in Kentucky, pastor at

Talladega College in Alabama, minister of an Atlanta-based church, and director of the Kentucky Commission on Interracial Cooperation. For several years, Jane Bond assisted the family on her teacher's salary. She pursued graduate studies at Oberlin College in sociology.

Horace's father relocated the family in constant search of employ-ment. Horace attended elementary and high schools at Lincoln Institute, Talladega College and Atlanta University. In 1919, Horace Bond com-pleted secondary school at the Lincoln Institute. In the fall of the same year, he entered Lincoln University, earning a B.A. degree in 1923. During the same year, he began his graduate studies at the University of Chicago. He earned a Master's Degree in Education in 1926 and was conferred a Ph.D. from Chicago concentrating in the history of educa-tion in 1936. One year later, the University of Chicago awarded him the *Susan Colver Rosenberg Prize* for the best thesis in social sciences titled "Social and Economic Influences on the Public School Education of Negroes in Alabama, 1865-1930." In 1939, Bond published his thesis as *Negro Education in Alabama: A Study in Cotton and Steel.*

Also during 1939, Dr. Bond became the first president of Fort Valley State College, where he served six years (1939-45). Bond continued the work of Henry Alexander Hunt that focused on teacher training for rural blacks. During his tenure as second principal of Fort Valley High and Normal School (1904-1938), Hunt paved the way to get state sup-port for the school. Donnie Bellamy noted in his book, *Light in the Valley,* "Principal Hunt thought the time was ripe for a move to get Georgia to take over the Fort Valley school as the State Agricultural College. Much debate ensued among school trustees, Chancellor S. V. Sanford and members of the Board of Regents about Hunt's proposal for the school. At that time, the American Church Institute's annual financial support was $15,000, and Hunt did not see any prospect of much inter-est from this source in increasing the amount. If the state would allocate $30,000 per year for support, Hunt believed that would be a good begin-ning. While the debate went on, the Fort Valley institution was in an unhealthy financial state." Hunt died on October 1, 1938 before reaping the fruit of his labor with this endeavor. Based on the foregoing, Bond was able to complete Hunt's dream of state support for the school and complete the transition. Using a gift from the Julius Rosenwald Fund, the Georgia Board of Regents acquired the Fort Valley school in June 1939, and made it a four-year unit of the University System. The name of the new senior college was changed to Fort Valley State College. FVSC experienced substantial growth during Bond's administration. For the first time, the college offered a Bachelor of Science degree in Home Economics. Dr. Bond conferred degrees to the first graduating class of 1941, which consisted of twenty-one students. Two more graduated during summer Commencement.

As president, Bond worked tirelessly to improve college-community relationships and to upgrade local black public schools. He also joined forces with the Conference of Presidents of Negro Land Grant Colleges and the United States War Department to plan vocational and academic training programs for black soldiers and veterans.

News about campus activities appeared in *The Peachite*, the official organ of student expression. This publication, established in 1943, provided a forum for newspaper staff to review an array of activities on the campus. One of the musical highlights of the year was the Choir's performance. The Annual Spring Recital delighted the college family and the community. In the same year, thousands of people throughout central Georgia turned their radio to Station WMAZ at 5 o'clock on Sunday afternoon to listen to the broadcast from the Fort Valley State College, sponsored by the Rhodes Furniture Company of Macon, GA. One of the few colleges in the country to host a regular broadcast, FVSC quickly enjoyed a reputation for presenting varied programs of wide interest and great educational value. The thirty-minute programs, were organized under the supervision of a special faculty Radio Committee consisting of President Horace Mann Bond, Dean W. W. E. Blanchet; J. Walker Freeman, Director of Music, Alma Stone, Instructor of Music; and Elaine E. Douglas, Instructor of English and Director of Dramatics. Students in the College Choir, the College Players' Guild, the Verse-Speaking Choir, various other student organizations, as well as numerous students from the general student body, participated in the broadcasts.

The Peachite also featured several annual events that drew large audiences: the College Choir's Easter Concert, Delta Sigma Theta Sorority's Mother's Day Program, Hubbard Day (dedicated to the memory and good works of William M. Hubbard, founder and president, State Teacher and Agricultural College at Forsyth, 1902-1939 and director of Public Relations, FVSC, 1939-1941); the Folk Day Festival held in connection with the popular Ham and Egg Show; Lyceum Series; Baccalaureate and Commencement.

The June 1943 edition of *The Peachite* focused on the President Bond's busy travel schedule during the Spring Quarter. The author noted that in addition to the Herculean task of administering college affairs, President Bond had an active schedule, attended numerous conferences in and out of state; delivered the Founder's Day address at Spelman College; gave the Annual Friedlander Lecture in Columbus, Georgia; spoke to the Atlanta Youth Conference on Citizenship; delivered a radio address entitled "What the San Francisco Conference Means to the Negro" and delivered seven high school and college Commencement addresses.

The newsletter also reported that by 1944, the college offered a degree in Agriculture. During that same year, FVSC conferred 50 degrees, the highest graduation rate in the school's history up to that time. The graduating class consisted of only two males due to WWII. Willie Boyd McNeil, *Peachite* reporter, noted that, "His (Bond's) belief that a student is educated by his activities outside as well as inside of the classroom walls was largely responsible for the Scope Chart, a plan improvised with the aid of the faculty by which a student may be judged for participation in extracurricular activities in order to qualify for graduation."

A man of many talents did not go unnoticed. The June, 1944 edition of the *The Peachite* noted that Dr. Bond accepted an invitation to be visiting professor in the Summer School of Northwestern University, Evanston, Illinois. He taught a course entitled, "The Negro in American Life," offered in the Garrett Theological Seminary of the Graduate

Religious Department at the university. Additionally, Dr. Bond and faculty members attended the Georgia Teachers and Educational Association in Atlanta, Georgia. Bond served as editor of "*The Herald*," the association's publication.

Author Donnie D. Bellamy noted that, "Under Bond's guidance the faculty committee on Curriculum Revision and Study developed a new device for evaluating the work of college students. This device, published in May 1945 under the title, *Measuring Objectives: A Manual and Guide*, attracted national attention from educators representing institutions of higher learning." Bellamy also stated that, "Horace Mann Bond received high marks as President of FVSC. In a 1942 U. S. Office of Education survey of black colleges, FVSC was praised as one of the few schools that had a "clear statement of purposes" and recognized that "it was serving a group of people who have special problems." As college president, Bond continued to publish, while simultaneously proving himself an imaginative and able administrator."

Historical Timeline: Dr. Horace Mann Bond, 1939–1945

1939 Dr. Horace Mann Bond appointed as first President at Fort Valley State College (FVSC)

1939 Georgia Board of Regents acquired Fort Valley Normal and Industrial School (named it the Fort Valley State College) and merged it with Forsyth Normal and Industrial School.

Mr. William M. Hubbard appointed Director of Public Relations

1940 Fort Valley Laboratory School (interim) established on the FVSC campus. Dr. C. V. Troup appointed as first principal

Dr. W. E. B. DuBois delivered the first Founders Day address on October 10 entitled, *The Significance of Henry Hunt.*

First Folk Festival featured famed trumpeter and Father of the Blues, William C. Handy, who served as chief judge.

1941 William Merida Hubbard died on March 21.

Cooperative houses erected and named in honor of William Merida Hubbard

Folk Festival combined with annual Ham and Egg Show

The first four-year college class graduated in June.

Henry A. Hunt High School established at FVSC in the Royal C. Peabody Building

1943   Inaugural publication of *The Peachite*, a quarterly student newspaper

Ham and Egg show featured in Life Magazine, March 22

Wartime Accelerated Commencement held on March 26 – six men graduated and called to military service; male graduates left for duty the day after graduation

Bond elected to serve as president of the Conference of Negro Land Grant Colleges

1944   Peabody Building damaged by fire, H. A. Hunt High School classes were held in barracks called "hutments," as well as in the Training School

Class of 1944 set a record for the largest graduating class (May 28, 1944) in the history of FVSC with fifty students

Dr. Horace Mann Bond resigned the presidency on June 30.

SOURCES: Donnie D. Bellamy, *Light in the Valley: A Pictorial History of Fort Valley State College since 1895* (Virginia Beach, Va.: Donning Company, 1996), 67, 68, 75, 77; *The Peachite* June 1943-1944 http://www.fvsu.edu/about/history

Academic Building
Photo courtesy FVSU Archives

Katye M. Troup
Photo courtesy Dan Archer

Cornelius and Katye Troup
Photo courtesy FVSU Archives

Chapter 4

First Lady Katye Murphy Troup
Served with Dr. Cornelius V. Troup, 1945-1966

I associate so many pleasant, nostalgic memories with Founders Day here at the Fort Valley State College. This is true because for 21 years of my husband's presidency at Fort Valley State College, it was always a joy for the Troup household to welcome the guest speaker to the president's home-and to the campus. This was coupled with joining the loyal, cooperative, members of the Fort Valley State College Family, in commemorating the founding of this institution, which, in its infancy, was a High and Industrial School.

Katye Murphy Troup
FVSC Founders Day Celebration, presentation of Dr. C. V. Troup's literary collection to FVSC, 1978

One of two children, Katye Murphy was born to Edward Wesley Murphy and Nina Matilda Lucas on June 20, 1906. She grew up in Waynesville, Georgia. She received her early education in the primary and secondary schools in Waynesville and Brunswick, Georgia. After high school graduation, she attended Morris Brown College, later transferred to Talladega College, earning a B. A. degree in elementary education. Upon graduation from college in 1927, she taught school for two years in the state of Georgia.

On June 20, 1931, Katye Murphy married Cornelius V. Troup. They became the parents of three sons, Cornelius V. Troup, Jr., Kenneth W. Troup and Elliott V. Troup.

The Troups with son, Kenneth, FVSC student
Photo courtesy Dan Archer

During an interview, Dr. Elliott V. Troup, her youngest son, shared an interesting bit of information. He said, "I would also relate that my father taught my mother in commercial studies while she matriculated at Morris Brown College."

Mrs. Troup and her husband moved to Fort Valley in 1939. He accepted the role as registrar at Fort Valley State College and served in various positions, including principal of FVSC Laboratory High School and Associate Professor in the Department of Education. Upon the resignation of FVSC President Horace Mann Bond, the Board of Regents appointed Dr. Troup as second president in 1945. Mrs. Troup's role as wife, mother and first lady required a lot of juggling; however, she served faithfully for more than two decades until her husband's resignation in 1966.

During their long tenure at FVSC, the Troups worked as a team and entertained many guests at the college. First Lady Troup accompanied Dr. Troup at Baccalaureate and Commencement services. They hosted receptions for new students, employees, Miss FVSC and her Royal Court at the President's residence. She also worked as secretary in the FVSC Department of Agriculture.

The *Flame* yearbook staff snapped photos of Mrs. Troup at events around campus. She always looked lovely, attired in gloves and hats at special events–Hubbard Day, Founders Day, Lyceum Series, and the annual Mother's Day dinner that she hosted for visiting mothers on the eve of graduation. Decked out in elegant gowns, she joined her husband for the crowning of Miss FVSC, Miss ROTC and Miss Summer School. The popular Ham and Egg Show always attracted large crowds to the college. The annual Thanksgiving Dinner became popular and was much anticipated by the first family, employees and students.

First Lady Troup and her husband were active members of Trinity Missionary Baptist Church. She served as a choir member and musical accompanist. On campus, the couple displayed their musical talent at special events. On one occasion, Dr. Troup played the piano and they sang a song that delighted the audience. The 1952 *Flame* noted that First Lady Troup engaged faculty and formed a choir, the Christmas Carol Singers. The purpose of the choir was to develop a spirit of camaraderie among faculty members of the college family. During the Yuletide season, The Christmas Carol Singers entertained audiences and created a festive spirit on campus.

Sunday evenings at Vesper were special for the college family. Dr. C. V. Troup delivered messages that faculty and students found to be inspirational and uplifting.

As previously noted, Dr. and Mrs. Troup had three sons. After graduating high school, Kenneth W. Troup attended FVSC. He was very active around campus, particularly in the Military Science Program. Kenneth was musically inclined and played the trumpet. The 1959 *Flame* yearbook featured Cadet Trumpeters that included Lieut. Col. Kenneth W. Troup. The following year, The *Flame* highlighted the Military Science Officers and noted Cadet Col. Kenneth Troup, senior cadet officer for 1958-60. Of course, other photos featured the proud parents with their son, Kenneth.

In addition to her extensive work on campus, First Lady Troup held active membership in Zeta Phi Beta Sorority, Inc., and appeared as guest speaker at events hosted by the organization. She was also affiliated with Sigma Shadows and the Ladies Auxiliary of Frontiers International.

After retirement, Dr. and Mrs. Troup relocated to Atlanta. She served faithfully at Friendship Baptist Church as a member of the King's Daughters, an auxiliary of the church, and the Uplifters Club. Mrs. Troup also volunteered regularly at the Sadie G. Mays Nursing Home.

Mrs. Troup's oratorical talents served her well. According to the October 20, 1978 edition of *The Peachite*, Mrs. Troup addressed faculty, staff and students at the annual Founders Day Celebration. On this occasion, she presented the literary works of her husband, Dr. C. V. Troup, to Dr. C. W. Pettigrew, fourth president. Here are excerpts from her speech:

When the decision was made to present Mr. Troup's literary collection to the college, as I began to peruse through his files, to compile the material to be presented today, my mind was refreshed, and I was again intrigued with the straightforwardness, the foresightedness, the relevancy and pertinence of his messages, his deep desire to inspire, to motivate each member of his audience, to higher and nobler goals and achievements and how he emphasized and re-emphasized to every Black man, woman, and child, the importance of cultivating a positive self-image. But none of his messages was complete without his admonishing those under the sound of his voice to invite God into their lives, and to choose, A Way of Life, the path of righteousness—difficult—But, oh so rewarding!

Among the referenced documents, Mrs. Troup shared a poem written by her husband that would inspire anyone. Mrs. Katye Murphy Troup died on June 5, 1984, at age seventy-seven.

A Friend

A friend is one who stands by you,
It matters not what you may do
A friend in health, a friend in pain
A friend in sunshine and in rain.
It matters not what life may bring,
A friend, to you, will always cling.
C. V. Troup

The Troups present special
guest, Dr. Martin Luther
King, Jr., in receiving line
Photo courtesy Albert O' Bryant

The Troup Family
Photo courtesy FVSU Archives

*SOURCES: Obituary, *The Peachite*, October 20, 1978, Vol. XXXVI, No.1; Interview with Dr. Elliott Troup 2011, Mrs. C. V. Troup, Sr.'s Presentation Speech-Founder's Day, October 10, 1978 (Homie Regulus Heritage Room, Henry A. Hunt Learning Resource Center, Fort Valley State University, Fort Valley, GA), 1952 Flame Yearbook; 1959 Flame Yearbook

Dr. Cornelius V. Troup
Second President, Fort Valley State College, 1945-1966
Photo courtesy FVSU Archives

In 1895, a group of broad-visioned White and Negro citizens of Fort Valley became dissatisfied with the type of schools that was operated for Negroes and decided to organize a new institution. Those founders were looking forward to the day the school at Fort Valley would offer wider educational opportunities to Negro youth. The broad visions of these founders, and of the late Henry A. Hunt and of Horace Mann Bond, have given to us and to generations yet unborn, a rich heritage.

Dr. C. V. Troup

Vesper Message, Fort Valley State College, Sunday, September 29, 1946
–"How Broad is your Vision?"

I am convinced that the time has come for us to take a long, hard look at what we are doing and how we are doing it, for I am sure all of us would agree that the day for "playing college" has passed. There is a crying need for service above and beyond the normal expectations.

President's Message to Faculty and Staff, Fort Valley State College, September 16, 1964

In 1945, Cornelius V. Troup replaced Horace Mann Bond becoming the second president of the Fort Valley State College. During his long tenure that spanned for twenty-one years, FVSC experienced phenomenal physical growth and academic progress.

Born in Brunswick, Georgia on February 7, 1902, Troup completed his elementary and secondary education at Risley Grammar School and Saint Athenasius High School in his hometown. He served as salutatorian of his high school graduating class. After graduating from high school in Brunswick, Troup entered Morris Brown College in Atlanta. He distinguished himself as an academician, musician, and debater. He completed the requirements for the Bachelor of Arts degree with honors in 1925. Upon graduation, he was retained at his alma mater as head of the commercial Department, a position he held from 1925 to 1927.

In 1928, Troup was appointed to his second professional position. He served as principal of Risley High School in his native Brunswick from 1928 to1939. In an assessment of Troup in June 1939, Horace Mann Bond remarked that he was "young, very able and intelligent." Bond also added that Risley High School was "probably the best high school in the state." Troup's work at Risley High School became a monument of achievement for many people. While serving as principal of Risley, Troup pursued graduate study at the University of Wisconsin, Columbia University, and Atlanta University. In 1937, the Atlanta institution conferred upon him the Master of Arts degree.

During the period 1939-1945, Troup held various positions including associate professor of education, registrar, and director of summer school at the Fort Valley State College. In 1940, he commenced his doctoral study at Ohio State University, studying as a Rosenwald Fellow. This university awarded him the Ph.D. degree in 1947, two years after his appointment as president of the Fort Valley State College. Troup was also honored by Wilberforce University and Morris Brown College. Both institutions conferred on Troup the LL.D degree, in 1949 and 1959, respectively.

Troup amassed a long list of accomplishments during his tenure as the second president. FVSC experienced a construction boom that resulted in new academic buildings and residential housing. New athletic facilities elevated school spirit and social life for students. Existing facilities were upgraded or renovated. For more than two decades, Troup and his wife Katye made a notable difference at FVSC, as described extensively in the Troup historical timeline.

In addition to performing his administrative duties as president, Dr. Troup became a member of various professional, social and civic organizations. He was a member of the American Association of Collegiate Registrars; the Association of Collegiate Deans and Registrars in Negro Schools; the Georgia Teachers and Educational Association, and the American Teachers Association. He was a member of Phi Delta Kappa and the Masonic Order. But, of all these organizations, he was most proud of his membership in the Phi Beta Sigma Fraternity, Inc. Some of his hobbies included reading, bridge, softball, tennis, music and raising poultry. Dr. and Mrs. Troup attended Trinity Missionary Baptist Church and were very active in the music and choral ministries.

Troup enhanced his distinction as author. His articles were published in the *Herald, Journal of Higher Education, Educational Leadership, University Administration Quarterly, Journal of Negro Education, Negro Educational Review, College and University Business,* and others. His book, *Distinguished Negro Georgians,* was published in 1962. His poems were published in such works as *Negro Voices, Music Unheard, Badge of Honor, and Ebony Rhythm.* Troup's poem below, *Believe in Yourself,* appeared in the *Sigma Light and Crescent Magazine,* published by Troup's fraternity, Phi Beta Sigma Fraternity, Inc.

Believe in Yourself

Believe in yourself, don't give up the fight
Just keep on struggling with all of your might,
Resolve that you will not yield in despair,
Your burdens, then, will be lighter to bear.

Believe in yourself then work doubly hard
To achieve your goal despite every odd.
Faith in one's self and the will to succeed
Are the requisites that all of us need.

Believe in yourself and be not dismayed!
Take courage from those who have made the grade.
Keep moving on with a resolute will
And you'll reach the top of life's rugged hill.
- Cornelius V. Troup

A Smile

What is it that makes life so cheery?
A smile, just a smile.
What lightens the heart, so worn, so weary?
A smile, just a smile.
How little it costs to give each day
A smile, just a smile!
'Twill help many a traveler on his way,
A smile, just a smile.
-Cornelius V. Troup

Historical Timeline: Dr. Cornelius V. Troup, 1945-1966

1945   Dr. Cornelius V. Troup appointed as second President of Fort Valley State College

1946   Veterans Unit constructed to house male students who served in WWI & WWII

1947   The Board of Regents adopted a resolution moving the Land-Grant designation from Savannah State College to the Fort Valley State College as the 1890 Land-Grant College for Negroes in Georgia.

Agriculture building (temporary structure) constructed to provide much needed offices and classrooms at the college

1948   John W. Davison Hall for women dedicated and named for first principal of Fort Valley High and Industrial School

1949   The Georgia General Assembly, in response to the Regents' resolution, officially designated The Fort Valley State College as the Land-Grant College for Negroes in Georgia.

1952   FVSC student Catherine Hardy won a gold medal as a member of the winning 400-meter women's relay team at the Olympic Games at Helsinki, Finland. Hardy previously set a world's record in 1951 for the 50-yard dash in New York City.

Anna T. Jeanes Hall (new facility) constructed as men's dormitory

The Henry Alexander Hunt Memorial Library (currently the Leroy Bywaters Building) dedicated on April 29

1953   The Home Management House for Home Economics, the Maintenance Warehouse for the Buildings and Grounds Department, the General Purpose Barn, the Farm Equipment Shed, and the Deep Well for the Division of Agriculture were made available for college use.

1954   Alva Tabor Agriculture Building constructed and named after Alva Tabor, Sr., "Head Itinerant Trainer for Negroes," who was honored for his key role in the formation of Negro FFA and the development of Camp John Hope.

        Henry A. Hunt High School, started in 1941 at FVSC, relocated to new site on Spruce Street.

1955   Bishop Dining Hall renovated

1957   William M. Hubbard Education Building dedicated, named after Hubbard, founder of the State Teachers and Agricultural College of Forsyth

        Dairy Barn completed

        Football Stadium (original) constructed

        FVSC was granted full membership in the Southern Association of Colleges and Schools (SACS). FVSC was among first of HBCUs to be admitted to the association.

        Graduate Division commenced

1958	College Laundry Building renovated, new equipment installed
1959	The George N. Woodward Health and Physical Education Building dedicated on December 11 and named after Woodward, long-time university physician, 1912-1946
1962	Peach County Training School renovated, renamed the Gano Building honoring a FVHI founder, F. W. Gano; building used for various FVSC programs
1963	Completion of Gano Annex
	The Isaac Miller Science Building dedicated on November 24, named after Miller, one of FVHI's founders.
1964	Sophia Moore Dormitory dedicated on October 10, named after Moore, FVSC's Supervisor of Custodial Services, 1908-1939 (FVNIS); 1939-1945 (FVSC)
1965	Anthony D. Watson Dormitory dedicated on November 21, named after Watson, Superintendent of Building and Grounds 1923-1939 (FVNIS); 1939-1946 (FVSC)
1966	The Henrietta Walden Myers Home Economics Building was completed, named after Myers, teacher of Arts and Crafts at FVHI, FVNIS and FVSC, 1916-1950.
	William Madison Boyd Hall opened, named after Boyd, a distinguished Professor of Social Science, 1940-1948
	Construction began on the Student Union Building.
	Dr. C. V. Troup retired as president on June 30.

SOURCES: Donnie D. Bellamy, *Light in the Valley: A Pictorial History of Fort Valley State College since 1895* (Virginia Beach, Va.: Donning Company, 1996), 89-93; http://www.fvsu.eduabout/history

Josephine D. Blanchet
Photo courtesy FVSU
Marketing Office

Waldo and Josephine Blanchet
Photo courtesy James Khoury

Chapter 5

First Lady Josephine Dorothy Lavizzo Blanchet Served with Dr. Waldo W. E. Blanchet, Sr., 1966-1973

It was at a high school dramatic presentation some years ago, in New Orleans, that Mr. Blanchet met his wife, the former Miss Josephine Dorothy Lavizzo. Being impressed by Miss Lavizzo, who was in the play, he asked to be introduced to her and the romance that was begun then, reached culmination on October 13, 1943, in Chicago, Illinois, where, amid simple rites, they were solemnly united in marriage.

Charles P. Cochran

Fort Valley State College, *The Peachite*, Volume III, Number 2, March 1945

Josephine Dorothy Lavizzo was born in New Orleans, Louisiana, on October 9, 1909, the third of nine children. She graduated from McDonogh 35 High School and Normal School where she trained and taught in the New Orleans Public School System. After some time, she moved to Chicago and secured a secretarial position in a real estate office. Later she established residency in Washington, D.C., and worked as a secretary also at the Pentagon. After years of separation, she reconnected and married Waldo W. E. Blanchet in 1943, the love of her life whom she knew previously in New Orleans.

A new life for Mrs. Blanchet began when she joined her husband, a long-time resident of Fort Valley. He started a new position in 1932 under Henry Alexander Hunt, second principal of Fort Valley High and Normal School. Hunt offered him a job as head of the Department of Science at the Fort Valley Normal and Industrial School. Dr. Blanchet served in this position from 1932-1936; became Dean in 1936 and served until 1938; promoted to Administrative Dean in 1939 and served until he was appointed as the third president of Fort Valley State College in 1966.

Josephine Dorothy Lavizzo Blanchet became the first lady at Fort Valley State College, and in every sense of the words, she was first a lady. She epitomized the qualities of poise, dignity, good taste, integrity, intelligence, and strength.

Mrs. Blanchet enrolled in the college and later graduated with honors and a degree in business education. She worked as part-time secretary for a number of years in the Home Economics Department before devoting herself full time to homemaking and duties as wife of the academic dean and eventually, the college's president. She spent quality time as a mother of two young children, Gerri and Waldo, Jr.

As first lady of the college, Mrs. Blanchet served as the official hostess. Annual campus events required her to entertain distinguished guests who attended Hubbard Day Convocations, Founders Day Observances and Lyceum series. The *Flame* yearbook staff included photos of the elegant first lady at the annual Miss FVSC's Coronation. First Lady Blanchet, along with the Queen's Royal Court, parents, relatives, students and staff anticipated the crowning of Miss FVSC by President Blanchet. This was just one of many exciting must-attend events hosted during Homecoming week. During the fall quarter, President and First Lady Blanchet greeted the freshman class by extending warm smiles and handshakes in a receiving line, followed by a reception. At the dedication of the new Food Service Center in 1972, President and First Lady Blanchet welcomed special guests, including retired dietician, Junia J. Fambro.

The Blanchet Family attended St. Juliana Catholic Church in Fort Valley. At FVSC, the Blanchets participated in the Newman Club, a Catholic student organization. First Lady Blanchet also spent quality time with members of The Fort Valley Chapter of The Links, Inc. Founded in 1946, The Links, Inc. is one of the oldest and largest volunteer service organizations of women who are committed to enriching, sustaining and ensuring the culture and economic survival of African Americans and other persons of African ancestry. Mrs. Blanchet and the Links chapter sponsored various projects that addressed cultural and educational needs of underserved families in the community. Many chapter members worked at FVSC.

During Dr. Blanchet's tenure as FVSC's president, the City and College were engaged in social, civil and racial unrest. Waldo recalled, "She (his mother) was quite an activist in her own way—be it at a drug store, refusing to answer when called by her first name, or refusing to go to the back of the store when directed by a sales clerk. She challenged every bigoted incident. Being a staunch supporter, she also opened her home to civil rights activists and marched and worked with her husband and FVSC students in support of much needed change during the turbulent sixties." However, the desegregation cases yield some positive results. For the first time in the city's political history, six black citizens challenged eleven whites for political positions in city government; only two of them were victorious. The College Family considered this to be a great achievement indeed for their noble efforts.

In 1972, Dr. Blanchet announced his retirement from Fort Valley State College.

The Presidential Reception hosted by FVSC became a crowning moment for Dr. and Mrs. Blanchet.

This excerpt taken from the 1966 *Flame* captured the event:
This year President and Mrs. W. E. Blanchet were honored by the faculty, staff, students and friends of the Fort Valley State College at a special banquet. The banquet was highlighted by remarks from friends present, and the reading of felicitations from friends, colleagues and former instructors. Their remarks were inspired by the unending efforts and contributions the Blanchets have made to the institution and the community for the past 37 years.

Sharing the occasion were special guests and members of Blanchet's family.

Among her friends, she became especially known for her New Orleans culinary skills. She excelled as an artist, exemplifying her impeccable taste and creativity in ways that included furniture design and restoration, interior design, gardening, sewing, embroidery, upholstery and crocheting. The game of bridge provided the social outlet for regular fellowship and gathering of close friends for years until she could no longer physically participate.

Mrs. Blanchet's close family ties, friendships and Catholic faith sustained her throughout life and in death on April 10, 2003, when she passed away at home with her children by her side. Mrs. Blanchet lived a good life and fought a good fight. Upon the end, Josephine Dorothy Lavizzo Blanchet said, somewhat in relief, "I've had everything in life I ever wanted. I am ready to go."

SOURCES: Dr. Waldo Blanchet, Ms. Geri Blanchet, 2011, *The Flame*, 1966, 1967, 1968, 1969 and 1972

Dr. Blanchet, First Lady Blanchet and Dr. John Dubriel
Photo courtesy Victoria Dubriel

Dr. Waldo W. E. Blanchet
Third President, Fort Valley State College, 1966-1973
Photo courtesy FVSU Archives

During these times of rapid social, economic, and political changes, it is most difficult to predict what the future will be. Although we cannot foresee the future, Fort Valley State College will be a part of it. The College will evaluate the changes that occur and revise its purposes to make them harmonize with those changes that it deems of sufficient value to influence its role in society.

A college should be a dynamic social institution and should strive to be of the greatest value to the largest number of people. Fort Valley State College must never be provincial in its outlook or static in its approach in clinging to the past and even the present in the face of the changing demands of society as a whole.

While no college should try to be everything to everybody, within the limits of its resources, Fort Valley State College should be responsive to requests for the services that it can provide. Then, too, Fort Valley State College, in its role as a service institution, must itself initiate activities and programs that will make life better in the immediate community and the larger community as well.

It is our hope that the students who attend Fort Valley State College will catch the spirit of community service and enter fully into the life of the community in which they live and into which they will go as graduates.

Dr. W. W. E. Blanchet

The Flame, President's Message, 1972

I deeply appreciate the character of the present student body, faculty and staff who despite the adverse publicity of this past summer have carried forward the business of education with vigor and high aspirations.

Dr. W. E. Blanchet

The Macon Telegraph, Ft. Valley's Dr. Blanchet to Retire, December 9, 1972

The Fort Valley State College has had a glorious history of service to Peach County, the State of Georgia, the nation and the world. While its immediate responsibility is to the students who are enrolled, the college extends its services to the community to the extent that the community wishes to avail itself of those services. The college's fundamental mission is to produce men and women of wisdom. While in college pursuing their studies, students are urged to make wise use of all the resources of the college to live a rational life while here. Upon completing their undergraduate and graduate studies, graduates are urged to apply the wisdom gained in the solution of problems they encounter in the communities in which they live. The activities of our alumni throughout the United States and in certain foreign countries bring credit to themselves and reflect the worth of the education that they acquired while at Fort Valley.

To the present generation of students and to all succeeding generations of students, may you live a life undergirded with wisdom in the choices that you make and filled with compassion for all who are less fortunate than you are.

Dr. W. E. Blanchet

The Flame, President's Message, 1973

Waldo William Emerson Blanchet succeeded Dr. C. V. Troup as the third president on July 1, 1966. Dr. Blanchet's career track in Fort Valley started in 1932 as Head of the Department of Science at the Fort Valley Normal and Industrial School. He became Dean in 1936 and later promoted to Administrative Dean in 1939. He was then appointed as third president of Fort Valley State College in 1966.

Dr. Blanchet, a native of New Orleans, attended Talladega College. He earned the B.A. degree in science in 1932, and studied, during the 1931-1932 school year, at the Atlanta University graduate school. In 1936, he received his M. S. degree in chemistry, at the University of Michigan, and studied for an additional semester there, the same year. During the summers of 1936 and 1937, he studied at the University of Chicago. In 1938-1939, he returned to the University of Michigan and studied for a full year. Blanchet resumed his studies at Michigan during the summers of 1939-1941 and the spring quarter of 1942. He ultimately completed all requirements for the Ph.D. degree at Michigan.

Author Donnie D. Bellamy, *Light in the Valley,* noted that, "When Dr. Blanchet took the helm of Fort Valley State College, the city and the college were enthralled in social, civil and racial unrest. Dr. Blanchet faced the issues firmly and openly. His speeches to the college faculty and students were published in both the college and city's newspapers." The new president's message delivered in September 1968 to the college reminded his listeners:

> There is a fertile field laboratory right here in Fort Valley and Peach County. We must make what we have available to the community. The City of Fort Valley, although relatively small, sustains most of the social ills of any other center of population.

While President Blanchet urged more political participation in Fort Valley and Peach County, he also encouraged students, faculty and staff members to become more active in governing the college.

Bellamy stated, "Two years later, after the social, civil, and racial unrest in the city left its impact on the College, the president's message remained unchanged. Blanchet became more forceful in advocating the community's role vis á vis the predominately black college." In his opening address for the academic year 1970-71, Dr. Blanchet asked the faculty and staff to "face the issues of the day:"

> Now I am not so blinded by idealism that I cannot see government, more properly politics, and the economy control almost everything including education. We might even reduce these two major influences to one by placing a hyphen between politics and the economy, for they go hand in hand.

Bellamy's book offered other intriguing details about this case. "The FVSC school desegregation case had its antecedent in hotly contested city and county elections and an undisguised political lawsuit. A reporter of the *Macon Telegraph* in July 1972 observed that the theme in Peach County politics that year was "fight shenanigans with shenanigans." In the 1972 Fort Valley city election, six blacks—the largest number in the political history of the city, challenged eleven whites for places in the city's government. Roosevelt Arnold, electrician and plumber, and Rudolph Carson, businessman, were the only black candidates who were victorious in the April regular election. Arnold won a place on the Utilities Commission. Carson defeated three white candidates for a City Council post." According to one Middle Georgia newspaper, "It was obvious college students . . . turned the trick for the black candidates."

Bellamy also observed, "Three of the remaining blacks received the highest number of votes for their respective posts, but failed to get a majority of the votes. The sixth black, who was in a pool of two blacks and three whites, came in fourth. The three blacks receiving the highest number of votes for their particular posts were in runoffs against white opponents Ed Dent, Newt W. Jordan, and Jack R. Hunnicutt. Although each black challenger was defeated in an April 19 runoff elections, each received a majority of the regular votes, but the results of the absentee ballots threw the election to their white opponents."

On another note, the student enrollment, approximately 1,600 at the time Blanchet became president in 1966, steadily increased to 2,071 in the fall quarter of 1972, but plummeted after the 1972 FVSC school desegregation case.

During Blanchet's presidency, the campus also experienced a boost in new construction. Students and employees welcomed the completion of Lottie M. Lyons Student Center, Cozy L. Ellison Building (agricultural mechanics), Florence Johnson Hunt Infirmary, Wilson-Roberts Building (physical plant) and Josephine Lewis Hall Dormitory.

In 1972, Blanchet made a special announcement to the college family. "After forty-one years of service at Fort Valley Normal and Industrial School and Fort Valley State College, I plan to retire at the end of the present year, June 30, 1973. After that many years of service, I think that I deserve a rest to travel and to write at leisure. I have known all of the graduates and former students of Fort Valley State College as teacher, dean or president. I touched in some way all graduates of Fort Valley Normal and Industrial School beginning with the fall of 1932 and the graduating class (high school and junior college) of 1933. I therefore, have a rich heritage of personal and professional associations with thousands of students and hundreds of faculty members over the years. For those associations, I shall be ever grateful to Fort Valley State College and the institution that was one of its forerunners."

"After you have labored as long as I have, I am sure that you, too, will welcome a rest and the time to do some of the things that you want to do and not those things that you are paid to do."

After receiving Blanchet's letter, Chancellor George Simpson, Jr. said, "I am reluctant to agree to President Blanchet's request to retire. He has done an excellent job in a difficult situation, and we are all in his debt."

Chairman W. Lee Burge of the Board of Regents said: "Dr. Blanchet has served the University System (of Georgia) and Fort Valley State well. We are sorry to lose him. Under Dr. Blanchet's leadership Fort Valley College had provided a most beneficial and educational opportunity at the college level for many of Georgia's citizens."

Blanchet retired on June 30, 1973.

Once again, the author found that Dr. Donnie Bellamy's overview of President Blanchet's tenure above was quite interesting. Although he experienced turbulent times, Blanchet persevered and made noble accomplishments at FVSC and in the Fort Valley community.

Historical Timeline: Dr. Waldo W. E. Blanchet, 1966–1973

1966   Dr. W. W. E. Blanchet appointed as third President at Fort Valley State College

1967   Lottie M. Lyons Student Union Building opened, named after Lyons, Dean of Women, 1944-1957

The Agricultural Mechanics Building opened

1969   Josephine Lewis Hall completed, named after Hall, sewing teacher, 1927-1928 and Resident Hall Director, 1935-1944

Wilson-Roberts Building (physical plant) completed, named after Wilson, Industrial Arts teacher, football coach, Assistant to Superintendent of Building and Grounds (Hunt High School 1940-41; Army 1941-44; resumed his career, 1944-1967) along with Roberts, Supervisor of Custodial Services (Fort Valley High and renamed Fort Valley Normal and Industrial School, Fort Valley State College), 1914-1966

New Faculty Housing completed

1970   H. A. Hunt High School, Spruce Street, closed as part of Peach County's desegregation plan. Peach County Schools were integrated by federal court into one high school and junior high.

1971   FVSC accredited by the National Council for the Accreditation of Teacher Education (NCATE)

1972   New Food Service Center opened

FVSC's first regionally televised football game appeared on ABC Television (FVSC vs. Fisk University at the Wildcat Stadium).

1973   Construction commenced on new Infirmary.

Dr. W. W. E. Blanchet retired as president and received Emeritus status.

SOURCES: Donnie D. Bellamy, *Light in the Valley: A Pictorial History of Fort Valley State College since 1895* (Virginia Beach, Va.: Donning Company, 1996), 93-97, 106; http://fvsu.edu/about/history

Academic Building
Photo courtesy FVSU Archives

Edwina Phinazee Pettigrew
Photo courtesy Beverly Hicks

Dr. Cleveland W. Pettigrew
Photo courtesy FVSU Archives

Chapter 6

First Lady Edwina Phinazee Pettigrew
Served with Dr. Cleveland W. Pettigrew, 1973-1982

On March 25, the college family bade farewell with chins up and in merry style to
twenty-six of our young men in the Enlisted Reserve Corp who were called to active
service. The Ambassadors played their best and the girls dressed in their loveliest
formals for the occasion. Soldiers from Camp Sheeler and Cochran Field were pres-
ent to help send-off and to welcome them in the uniforms of the Armed Services.
Brave women of the hour were...Edwina Phinazee...
The Peachite, *Vol. 1, No. 1, June 1943*

Edwina Phinazee is playing the orthophone and looks as if her mind is far away.
Wonder if she is wishing for someone, or just thinking of previous Barn Dances.
Now Lucille Collins is looking at Edwina. Perhaps she will go over and tell her not
to worry because the boys (male students drafted into armed forces) will be home
again soon to join in the fun.

Esther N. Lewis

The Peachite, *"A Whirl in the Social World," Vol. II, No. 3, June 1944*

The friends of Miss Edwina Phinazee surprised her with a birthday party in the
reception room of Huntington Hall, Friday night, November 13. Her friends hid
in the dark reception room until she arrived. She was completely surprised when
the lights were turned on and she was congratulated.

Olive G. Williams

The Peachite, *"A Whirl in the Social World," Vol. III, No. 1, Dec.1944*

Edward David and Lena Kelsey Phinazee welcomed the birth of Edwina on
November 18, 1922. The first of three children, she spent her childhood in
Waynesboro, Georgia. As a result of loving and steadfast parental influences,

she grew into an extremely kind and giving person, free of contention, yet possessing a quiet resolve.

She attended elementary and secondary schools in Waynesboro, Georgia. After graduating from high school, she enrolled at Fort Valley State College. While studying to become a primary school teacher, she met her future husband, Cleveland W. Pettigrew. She graduated in spring 1944 and was conferred a bachelor's degree in education. This class of 50 set a record for the largest graduating class in the history of Fort Valley State College at that time.

Margaret Wilson McCormick offered reflections about her classmate, seventy-two years after they entered FVSC during the fall quarter, 1940. Mrs. McCormick described Edwina as quiet, pleasant, and attractive; but she was also popular around campus. During the summer, she recalled, "Edwina assisted with the family funeral home in her hometown, Waynesboro Georgia. She developed a strong bond with students who also came from families that operated funeral homes." "The college was always bustling with activities sponsored by campus organizations," she noted. She further elaborated, "Students enjoyed many traditional events-Hubbard Day, Folk Festival, Ham and Egg Show, Founders Day, Homecoming Week and performances sponsored by the College Choir and Players Guild each quarter. Everyone tuned in to FVSC's weekly radio broadcasts and student performances aired by WMAZ. Students wore their Sunday attire and attended Lyceum Series, Vesper Service and the much-anticipated Thanksgiving meal in the dining hall. During the spring season, it was customary for beautiful young ladies to compete for a special title, the Peaches of FVSC. They strolled into the orchards when the trees were in bloom to have their photos taken. After the contest, Miss Peach Bloom and seven attendants made their debut. *The Peachite*, student newspaper, and *The Flame* yearbook featured many of these photos." Yes, Mrs. McCormick recalled fondly the experiences she shared with Edwina from the good ole days at FVSC.

After graduating college, the long courtship with Cleveland, which had begun in the early 1940s, came to fruition when Edwina married him on his return from service in World War II. After marriage, she began a long life of service as a wife, mother and educator. The couple became the proud parents of three children; one daughter, Beverly and two sons, Roderic and Darrell.

Mrs. Pettigrew taught second grade at elementary schools in Waynesboro, Baxley, Griffin and Albany, Georgia. She continued her professional education by enrolling in graduate studies at Indiana University. She later taught at Chattahoochee and Grant Park schools in Atlanta. It was over the course of these years that she had the greatest impact on her pupils as she helped to build character, morality and excellence in their lives.

When Dr. Pettigrew became president of Fort Valley State College in 1973, she assumed the role as first lady at her alma mater. Mrs. Pettigrew assisted her husband by cultivating relationships with downtown merchants in Fort Valley. She attended many annual events hosted at the college —Ham and Egg Breakfasts, Miss FVSC Coronation and Balls, Homecoming festivities, Lyceum Series, Founders Day Observances, Commencements, Hunt, Bond, Troup Banquets, Open House and Parents Days and Honors Convocations. During their ninth year at FVSC, her husband died unexpectedly of a heart attack in 1982.

The *Flame* 1983-84 yearbook staff dedicated this volume to Dr. C. W. Pettigrew. Photos included a memorial service before a capacity crowd in the Woodward Gym. On this occasion, Dr. Pettigrew's family listened attentively as faculty, staff and community members paid tribute to him. Dr. Maceo Pettigrew, the president's brother, also presented a donation to the Pettigrew Endowment Fund established in support of student scholarships.

Before his death in 1982, Dr. Pettigrew's brainchild envisioned the implementation of new programs aimed to create a diverse student body. Sanctioned by the Board of Regents, this project fulfilled, in part, the 1978 FVSC desegregation plan to attract the non-traditional audience to campus that would provide the setting for many outreach programs in the middle Georgia community.

In 1987, Mrs. Pettigrew, along with family, friends and the FVSC Family, attended the dedication ceremony of the C. W. Pettigrew Farm and Community Life Center on June 5. During the program, William T. Pendergrass, artist, unveiled a portrait of Dr. Pettigrew that's located in the foyer. The Rev. Maceo Pettigrew, brother of late C. W. Pettigrew, and Mrs. Pettigrew joined President Luther Burse in the ribbon cutting ceremony to formally establish the C.W. Pettigrew Endowment Fund mentioned previously. After the ceremony, guests enjoyed refreshments, music and tours of the new facility. The 55,000 square-foot conference/convention/fine arts facility provides outreach services to the Fort Valley State University community. It houses the center's Administrative Offices and the Fort Valley State University Cooperative Extension Program. Pettigrew Center facilities are available to individuals, groups and organizations for educational, cultural, business, civic and public service functions or private parties. The 600-seat performing arts theater can enhance any organization's large meeting needs. The high-tech sound system, acoustics and computerized lighting equipment make the theater one of the finest in the area.

C.W. Pettigrew Farm and
Community Life Center
Photo courtesy FVSU Archives

Unveiling of
Dr. Pettigrew's portrait
Photo courtesy FVSU Archives

One year after his death, the FVSC Family and friends hosted a symposium entitled, "Save the Goose that Lays the Golden Egg: The Legacy of Cleveland William Pettigrew as College President," held on February 25. A Steering Committee of college staff and individuals in the community planned a daylong forum that focused on Dr. Pettigrew's accomplishments and essential projects to be completed by the new administration. The committee assembled an impressive group of presenters – University System of Georgia Chancellor, president of St. Augustine's College, FVSU alums and university administrators. In addition, local officials in Fort Valley made presentations along with comments by the Pettigrew Family.

Mrs. Pettigrew's family shared a personal story about her nickname. She became affectionately known as "Coconut" by her husband because at times she exhibited such strong will and determination that her head was likened to being as hard as a coconut. This nickname remained with her throughout her life.

Writings, which characterize her warm and loving personality and the deep adoration she enjoyed from her family were expressed to her in personalized greetings on Mother's Day, 1993:

"As long as I have known you it has been Mother's Day. I do not need a day to tell you how much you mean to me."
"No one could ever have a better mother or grandmother! You raised us right!"
"Coconut, we are blessed with the best." "I love you. Of all the qualities you have, I appreciate most your kindness."
"You're the best grandmother and I love you very much. You make me happy because you are always doing things for me to make sure I am happy."
"To the grandmother who was there when I came into the world, may I grow up to be like you."

Edwina Phinazee Pettigrew died on August 2, 1993, in Atlanta, GA at age seventy-one.

SOURCES: Obituary, Interview with Margaret McCormick 2012, *The Flame Yearbook* 1983-84, *The Peachite 1943, 1944*

Dr. Cleveland W. Pettigrew
Fourth President, Fort Valley State College, 1973-1982
Photo courtesy FVSU Archives

Through the continued and sustained help of our several publics—local community, distant, interested friends, parents, the news media committed to fair reporting and, of course, through; students and alumni, "The Fort Valley State College Story" must be told over and over and over again - until all vestiges of biases, half-truths and misconfigurations fade into rightful insignificance, and the true reflection of this institution's worth and contributions is projected once more as the Magnificent Mother she is known to be in the lives and work of all whom she has touched. For these graduating members of the class of 1974; such is to be your challenge; many are to be your rewards. God bless you and keep you strong!

Dr. C. W. Pettigrew

The Flame (1973-74, The President's Message)

My dear Students, Faculty and Friends:
It is not too often these days that college presidents are invited to write a letter to their student bodies in student publications. In fact, this is the first time I have been so provided the opportunity, and I express appreciation to Editor McNeil, Advisor Gipson, and Mrs. Karen Smith for the chance it affords. Now, there are

a few important things I feel I should say. First, let me share with you some items about your college. If you have come to FVSC within the last three (3) years, you were admitted through a far tougher screening process than your predecessors. In fact, eighty-nine (89) applicants this year were refused admission due to low academic preparation alone! Additionally, forty (40) students have been dropped for deficient academic averages. These actions take on further significance when it is understood that under the present funding formula used in the University System, a smaller head-count translates into fewer operational dollars. But such an action on the part of administration, faculty and students serves notice that they were united in a determination that an already strong FVSC degree grows increasingly competitive each passing year.

Secondly, let me recognize the role of the FVSC faculty in preparing itself quarterly through well-planned and implemented institutes to coordinate resources and people toward the end of ever-broadening curricular programs and instructional activities. Their dedication is reflected in start-up programs as Ornamental Horticulture, Computer Science Technology, Historical Preservations, Economics, and Early Childhood Education in addition to those of Criminal Justice, Electronics Technology, Agribusiness and Animal Health Technology.

And finally, this is HC (Homecoming)!!! Enjoy yourselves well, but deport yourselves well – as I know you do in 97.8 percent of the cases! And help us make all of our alumni and friends to feel welcomed and appreciated.

C. W. Pettigrew

The Peachite, President's Letter, Friday, November 14, 1980

Cleveland W. Pettigrew, son of Addie Cody Pettigrew and James Oscar Pettigrew was a native of Scotland (Telfair County), Georgia. He demonstrated leadership qualities at an early age. As a young man, he was elected president of his class at Center High School in Waycross, Georgia, and later also of his graduating class at Fort Valley State College.

He received the Bachelor of Science degree from FVSC in 1945; after further study, Pettigrew also earned a master's degree at Atlanta University and his Doctor of Education degree at Cornell University in 1957.

During his career, he held a variety of administrative positions, including high school principal, and on the college level, head of the education department, director of public relations, and acting Dean of Instruction. Institutions where he served included Brooks High School, Fairmont High School, Edward Waters College, Albany State College, Alabama State College, Elizabeth City State Teachers College, South Carolina State College and Atlanta University.

Dr. Pettigrew returned to Fort Valley State College in 1961 as professor of education. He was later named the Dean of Graduate Studies, and by 1973 he became the third president, and first alumnus to be president of The Fort Valley State College.

Faculty members who served during Dr. Pettigrew's presidency remember fondly the faculty meetings during which he presided, cajoling the faculty and talking to the members about matters that concerned them and the college. [According to Anna Holloway, who was Assistant Professor of English during those years.]

Dr. Pettigrew received numerous honors. The National Institute of Mental Health selected him as a post-doctoral research fellow. In 1973, FVSC honored Pettigrew as Alumnus of the Year. Two years later, he was listed in the 1975 edition of *Notable Americans.*

Dr. Pettigrew served as a member of the Board of Directors of the Middle Georgia Private Industry Council and Warner Robins Air Logistics Center Equal Opportunity Committee. He was elected president of the Georgia Association of Colleges and also appointed to the Governor's Committee on Public Higher Education Finance.

As FVSC president, his accomplishments were many. Under his administration, six new buildings that enhanced student services opened. Among the renovated projects, Founders Hall and the east wing of Jeanes Hall were completed. Also, FVSC advanced to Division II of the National Collegiate Athletic Association. Additionally, new programs were approved in the areas of Psychology, Political Science, Criminal Justice, Agricultural Economics, Computer Scienc, and Electrical Engineering.

Before his death in 1982, Dr. Pettigrew had a vision that a community center, made available to the area residents and the people of the State of Georgia, would promote diversity at the college. His vision was funded as part of the 1978 desegregation plan of the University System of Georgia. The plan was refined, and two facilities were built. The Houston Stallworth Agricultural Research Building was dedicated in 1984. Three years later, the C. W. Pettigrew Farm and Community Life Center opened in 1987 and has been recognized as Dr. Pettigrew's legacy. Although he did not live to see his vision become a reality, many individuals eagerly awaited the completion of a facility that would serve residents in middle Georgia and the State of Georgia.

Historical Timeline: Dr. Cleveland W. Pettigrew, 1973-1982

1973   Dr. Cleveland W. Pettigrew appointed as fourth president at Fort Valley State College

First acquisition of property on State College Drive

1974   Huntington Hall renovated for administrative offices

Poultry Research Center completed

1975   New Florence Hunt Infirmary opened

Sophia Moore Hall annex completed

1976   Henry Alexander Hunt Memorial Library opened

Horace Mann Bond Building dedicated

Academic Building renamed Founders Hall as a tribute to the institution's founders

Memorial Towers dedicated to Henry A. Hunt, second principal of Fort Valley High and Industrial School/ Fort Valley Normal and Industrial School; Horace Mann Bond, first president of Fort Valley State College; and Cornelius Vanderbilt Troup, second president

1978   The College was accredited by the Engineering Council for Professional Development/ Accreditation Board of Engineering and Technology (ECPD/ABET).

The O'Neal Veterinary Technology Building constructed, named to honor Otis S. O'Neal, Negro County Agent, agricultural teacher (1910-1950), and founder of the nationally acclaimed "Ham and Egg Show"

Pettigrew inducted into FVSC Alumni Hall of Fame

1979   The Leroy Bywaters Business Building (previously the Hunt Library) was renovated to house the Department of Business and Economics and named after Bywaters, FVSC Business Manager/Comptroller and athletic coach, 1939-1965.

The Agricultural Mechanics Building dedicated, named after Cozy L. Ellison who served FVSC for 31 years in various roles including instructor and professor of Agriculture; Deputy Director of Cooperative Research

Perimeter Road (from State College Drive to Carver Drive) renamed Memorial Drive, honoring those persons who made contributions to FVSC for whom a building may never be named

FVSC accredited by the American Association of Veterinary Medicine

Fort Valley State College's first *Fact Book* was published.

1981   The circle at the front entrance of campus named College Circle

1982   Houston Stallworth Research Center construction commenced

Dr. Cleveland W. Pettigrew suddenly died of a heart attack while in office, June 11. Dr. Walter W. Sullivan appointed as acting president, served through August 1983

SOURCES: Donnie D. Bellamy, *Light in the Valley: A Pictorial History of Fort Valley State College since 1895* (Virginia Beach, VA: Donning Company, 1996), 106-107; http://www.fvsu.edu/about/history; Obituary 1982.

Academic Building
Photo courtesy FVSU Archives

Mamie B. Burse
Photo courtesy
FVSU Archives

Luther and Mamie Burse
Photo courtesy FVSU Archives

Chapter 7

First Lady Mamie Balbon Burse
Served with Dr. Luther Burse, 1983-1988

Dr. Donnie Bellamy, FVSU Professor Emeritus, noted that "when Mrs. Mamie Burse arrived with her husband, Dr. Luther Burse, the fifth president of Fort Valley State College, it appeared she had come home. She had a burning desire to become involved in college and community activities." Dr. Bellamy surmised that "her youthful appearance and thinking likely boosted students' enthusiasm and promoted school spirit."

Mamie Balbon Burse grew up in Virginia Beach, Virginia. Her parents loved and nurtured six children, two sons and four daughters. After early educational, social and spiritual preparation, she entered Elizabeth City State University, Elizabeth City, North Carolina, where she earned a B.A. degree in Physical Education. Later, she earned a M.A. degree at Cheyney State University, Cheyney, Pennsylvania, specializing in Supervision and Administration. Mrs. Burse pursued further studies at the University of Maryland at College Park, University of Delaware and Trinity College, Washington, D.C.

Dr. Luther Burse was appointed the fifth president of Fort Valley State College in 1983. Mrs. Burse and her husband settled in Fort Valley along with their daughter, Elizabeth. Their son, Luther, Jr., was already enrolled at Morehouse College. The family attended Trinity Missionary Baptist Church and their daughter participated in various youth programs.

Upon her arrival, she secured employment with the Peach County Senior Citizens Center. Being a trained educator, Mrs. Burse later served as assistant principal at Crawford County Middle School, Roberta, Georgia.

As the parent of a middle school student, she served as a volunteer with the Peach County Public School system where her daughter, Elizabeth, was involved in extracurricular activities. Being agile and filled with school spirit, she also joined the cheerleader squad in High School.

Of course, there were other school activities: PTO meetings, special events and parent-teacher conferences that kept Mrs. Burse involved.

During her tenure as first lady at FVSC, Mrs. Burse became involved in many college activities. Berry and Cheryl Jordan, friends of First Lady Burse, recalled that, "They worked together as members of the End Zoners Club." Chartered in 1978, the club membership included alums, faculty, staff and community supporters. The club hosted fundraisers that supported all athletic teams at FVSC. During home games, the club managed the concession stands. Of course, First Lady Burse also entertained guests in the President's box at Wildcat Stadium. During the fall quarter, the End Zoners hosted its annual picnic that delighted athletes, cheerleaders and band members; First Lady Burse also assisted. She often served as chairman of the Annual End Zoners Athletic Recognition Banquet. As a reward of their labor, Berry and Cheryl stated that, "The club used funds to purchase a 15 passenger van for the Athletic Department, ice machine for the field house, and new uniforms for all athletes." They noted that on another occasion, "First Lady Burse coordinated the construction of a donation box with employees in the Plant Operations Division." On game days, fans supported FVSC athletics with their donations. The May 2, 1986 edition of *The Peachite* listed other activities implemented by the End Zoners: purchased championship rings for the 82-83 football Team, renovated stadium seats, installed a new football goal post and contributed funds toward the purchase of baseball uniforms. The club hosted and co-sponsored several SIAC Women's basketball championship tournaments and also provided financial assistance to FVSC athletic teams upon request. The new communication system for the coaching staff was welcomed along with new uniforms donated to the basketball and tennis teams. New tennis rackets were also purchased and appreciated. President and First Lady Burse also attended out of town games to support the Wildcats.

As you would imagine, other responsibilities kept her on the fast track. President and First Lady Burse hosted receptions annually that welcomed new students to FVSC. The Burses greeted students, alumni and community supporters at annual events such as Ham and Egg Breakfasts; Miss FVSC Coronation and Balls; Homecoming festivities; Lyceum Series; Founders Day Observances; Hunt, Bond, Troup Banquets; Open House and Parents Days; Banks, Pierro, and Rutland Banquets; ROTC Balls and Honors Convocations; just to name a few. Additionally, she attended receptions hosted by the college during Black History Month observances. Further, First Lady Burse participated as a volunteer in the annual Blood Drives sponsored by the American Red Cross at FVSC. In recognition for hosting four blood drives annually, the college received a plaque in 1988 from the American Red Cross.

On one special occasion in December, President and First Lady Burse expressed their appreciation to faculty and staff at an affair hosted at the Women's Club, located in Fort Valley. The Christmas Gala delighted their guests at this historic home built in 1924 with beautiful features: crystal chandeliers, fireplaces with hand carved mantels and antique furnishings.

Students benefited from her involvement with campus-based organizations, and faculty welcomed her time and talents devoted to committees that promoted the college. For her dedication and resourcefulness, Fort Valley State College and the community showered her with an abundance of love and respect.

When Dr. Burse resigned as FVSC's president in 1988, the Burses relocated to Upper Marlboro, Maryland.

Mamie Burse
Photo courtesy FVSU Archives

The Burse Family
Photo courtesy FVSU Archives

SOURCES: Resume, *The Peachite*, May 2, 1986

Dr. Luther Burse
Fifth President, Fort Valley State College, 1983-1988
Photo courtesy FVSU Archives

Fort Valley State College is a product of its founders' desire to honor and transmit a legacy, but also to change and improve a people. Today as students and the beneficiaries of their great gift you must see today's changes as opportunities to shape tomorrow. As members of the Fort Valley State College Family, you cannot avoid the reality of your impact on the destinies of future generations. Therefore, you must not only value and understand the necessity for change as you prepare for your ultimate roles in life; you must also embrace the self-improvements that are fundamental to a strong future for all of us.

Luther Burse

The Flame, 1983-84

This mini report of the current state of affairs at Fort Valley State College should provide a better understanding of our college, our people, our accomplishments and our needs.
The total enrollment for the current quarter is 1,870. This represents an increase of 136 students, 8 percent over the enrollment of the 1982 fall quarter. The Financial Aid Office has awarded more than 1,700 of these students financial assistance in excess of $3 million.

Our increased enrollment created a shortage of housing for female students and required temporary space adjustments in several dormitories to accommodate the overflow. On a bright note, the resultant increase in revenue from student activity fees has enabled us to expand the cultural, educational and recreational programs provided within the college Student Activity Program Series.

Luther Burse

The Peachite, December 2, 1983

In the fall of 1983, Dr. Luther Burse took office as fifth President of the Fort Valley State College, following the death of President C.W. Pettigrew. Burse, his wife Mamie and their two children, Luther Jr. (enrolled at Morehouse College) and Elizabeth, quickly blended into the college family. Like both of his predecessors and his successors, Burse was well qualified for the FVSU position. He earned a baccalaureate degree from Kentucky State University, a master's degree from Indiana University and doctorate from the University of Maryland at College Park. His teaching and administrative experience included positions at Elizabeth City State in North Carolina and Cheney State College in Pennsylvania. While at Cheney, he served as coordinator of graduate studies and interim president. He guided Fort Valley State College through a time of tremendous growth and development. The college's appearance on the national scene was heightened by a visit from ABC's *Good Morning America* in the year following Burse's arrival.

One of the most noteworthy advancements of the Burse years was the start of the Cooperative Developmental Energy Program with seed money from the U.S. Department of Energy. This program, directed by Dr. Isaac Crumbly, allowed students to study at FVSC and also at a variety of other universities, including the University of North Las Vegas, Nevada. This initiative allowed students to complete degrees in mathematics and engineering and move to careers in the energy industry. Known as CDEP, the program, which continues today, has received continuing funding from a number of energy corporations and has become a signature Fort Valley State initiative.

Other advancements during the Burse years included the initiation of the Academic Honors Program developed to provide special classes for students with the top academic preparation; the first provision of courses in Computer Science and Electronic Engineering Technology at the Robins Air Force Base; the dedication of the C.W. Pettigrew Farm and Community Life Center, which provided FVSC with a conference center, and the opening of the Georgia Small Ruminant Research and Extension Center as part of the institution's Land Grant and agricultural mission.

Dr. Burse left the Fort Valley State College in 1988, and Dr. Melvin E. Walker, Jr., took over as acting president. Burse had overseen much growth and expansion and left the institution poised to move toward new heights. He initiated efforts to acquire university status.

Historical Timeline: Dr. Luther Burse, 1983-1988

1983   Dr. Luther Burse appointed as fifth President at Fort Valley State College, beginning on September 1

1984   The Stallworth Agricultural Research Building opened, named for Houston Stallworth, Professor of Horticulture and chairman, Division of Agriculture, 1945-1978

1985   Goat Research Complex completed and renamed The Georgia Small Ruminant Research and Extension Center

The U. S. Congress under Section 1416 of the Food Security Act of 1995 authorized funding for enhancement of Agricultural extension facilities at 1890 institutions and Tuskegee Institute.

Fort Valley State College appeared on ABC TV's *Good Morning America,* on May 16.

1986   Bachelor of Science Degree in Veterinary Science initiated

Academic Honors Program initiated

1987   Approval received and a memorandum of understanding signed for Fort Valley State College to offer Electronic Engineering Technology courses at Robins Air Force Base, Warner Robins, Georgia

The C. W. Pettigrew Farm and Community Life Center dedicated, named after Cleveland W. Pettigrew, Dean of the Graduate Division and fourth president of Fort Valley State College

The Georgia Small Ruminant Research and Extension Center, under the auspices of the Agricultural Research Station, became fully operational.

Bishop Hall was renovated to serve as the new Mass Communications building

1988   Dr. Luther Burse resigned as president.

1988   Dr. Melvin Walker appointed at acting president

SOURCES: Donnie D. Bellamy, *Light in the Valley: A Pictorial History of Fort Valley State College since 1895* (Virginia Beach, Va.: Donning Company, 1996), 108, 115-117; http://www.fvsu.edu/about/history

Jacqueline P. Prater
Photo courtesy FVSU Archives

Oscar and Jacqueline Prater
Photo courtesy FVSU Archives

Chapter 8

First Lady Jacqueline Polson Prater
Served with Dr. Oscar L. Prater, 1990 – 1998

I hope to see the Jacqueline The First Lady 1995 (namesake daylily) become a perennial reminder of a truly great lady for everyone who visits the Fort Valley State University campus.

Dr. Johnny Carter
FVSU Professor of Horticulture (Retired)

My memory of Jacqueline Prater still remains fresh as if she is still here with us today. I forgot who invited Mrs. Prater, but I met her at our early Central Georgia Pan African Festival (now Pan African Festival of Georgia). I actually remember where she sat (directly across from me in the Tubman African American Museum board room, upstairs).

Jacqueline was always on time. Most of the time, she would arrive all the way from Fort Valley before some folks from Macon. During the general meetings, she would contribute and share her thoughts freely and unreservedly. On the day of the festival, Mrs. Prater would be among the first to arrive early at the Central City Park for set up and stayed late for breakdown.

At a personal level, we had long conversations about heritage and self-esteem. Without a doubt, Jacqueline had a healthy dose of self-confidence. She knew who she was and whose she was. I will forever remember Jacqueline as a woman whose smile, energy and vibrancy filled every space and every room. We could count on her to do what she committed to doing. She exemplified the principles of the festival: love, peace, unity, and hope.

Needless to say that the news of her death deeply saddened us; and I have no doubt that she is resting with God.

Chi Ezekwueche, November 2012

Jacqueline Celestine Polson was born August 21, 1939, to parents Grady and Thea Polson in Christchurch, Virginia. She received her early education in the public schools of Middlesex County, Virginia. Mrs. Prater's mother, and cousin, Inez D. Jones, provided her formal music instruction. Additionally, Audrey B. Robinson and George Howell of Richmond, Virginia, taught her piano and organ. After graduating from high school, she attended Hampton University earning a B.S. degree in music education.

Mrs. Prater entered graduate school and received a Master of Music degree in music education from the Boston Conservatory of Music. While at the Conservatory, she composed and produced an operetta for grades one through seven entitled *A Miracle of Spring*. Mrs. Prater served as a music educator for thirty-six years.

Mrs. Prater spent her early years as a member of Calvary Baptist Church in Christchurch where she served as organist and in later years at St. Mark's Congregational Church in Boston. Additionally, she was organist and choir director at the historic First Baptist Church in Williamsburg, Virginia. An accomplished musician, she gained recognition on the national level as a renowned organist in Boston and as pianist for the Boston Conservatory Choir.

Mrs. Prater and her husband, Dr. Oscar Lewis Prater, joined the Fort Valley State College family in 1990. The Board of Regents of the University System of Georgia appointed Dr. Prater as sixth president.

As first lady of Fort Valley State University, Mrs. Prater fostered positive relations throughout the local community. The first family joined Trinity Missionary Baptist Church where Mrs. Prater was very active with the music ministry. The Peach County High School benefitted from her service as choral director. Mrs. Prater touched thousands of young people's lives through music, her passion.

She served as accompanist for many activities and events including those sponsored by Fort Valley area churches, the Peach Area Civic Theater and the Peach Festival Chorus. First Lady Prater also served as a member of the FVSC Pipe Organ Committee. The committee's original goal was to raise $50,000 for restoration of the college's pipe organ, but later increased by $10,000 due to inflation and delayed startup.

The small ten-rank Reuter organ was initially installed at Founders Hall in 1969. FVSC was among few colleges in the U.S. that owned pipe organs. During the renovation of Founders Hall, however, the organ sustained much damage. The committee was determined to raise money and restore the organ. The theme, *Pipe Dreams:* Help Save the FVSC Pipe Organ started the drive. FVSC also partnered with Piggly Wiggly, Corp. and made a public appeal to shoppers by requesting them to save labels marked distributed by Piggly Wiggly, Corp., Memphis, TN. Supporters were asked to mail or deliver labels to the Pettigrew Center. Over a period of four years, the committee successfully raised funds to restore the organ that was moved to a new location, C. W. Pettigrew Farm and Community Life Center. The dedication ceremony held on November 3, 1994 started FVSU's Centennial Celebration. First Lady Prater and other musicians performed at the Choir Concert and Pipe Organ Recital held in the Pettigrew Center.

First Lady Prater with the Pipe Organ Committee
Photo courtesy FVSU Archives

As a part of the FVSC's 100-year celebration in 1995, Jacqueline Prater also presented an original composition titled "A Centennial Hymn" to the school's archives.

A CENTENNIAL HYMN

By Jacqueline Prater, Fort Valley State College's First Lady

(Refrain)

A richer heritage, a brighter future;
Fort Valley State, you answered the call.
For one hundred years you did endure;
Fort Valley State, you're still standing tall.
One hundred years, one hundred years;
Fort Valley State, you're still standing tall.

(1st Verse)

You answered the call; you're still standing tall,
A miracle did unfold, your history took hold.
As we pass through your doors, your mission still soars.
You've blessed us all, one hundred years.
Fort Valley State, you've blessed us all.

(2nd Verse)

A vision with love bred a dream so true,
Eighteen fine men, a miracle did unfold.
With principles strong and faith in God, too,
Fort Valley State your history took hold.
One hundred years, one hundred years,
Fort Valley State your history took hold.

(3rd Verse)

The years did come and the years did go,
As teachers and scholars passed through the doors,
And knowledge and learning continue to flow;
Fort Valley Sate, your mission still soars.
One hundred years, one hundred years,
Fort Valley State, your mission still soars.

(Refrain)

A richer heritage, a bright future;
Fort Valley State, you answered the call.
For one hundred years, you did endure
Fort Valley State, you've blessed us all.
One hundred years, one hundred years;
Fort Valley State, you've blessed us all.

The Flame yearbook featured photos of First Lady Prater at various events around campus including Homecoming festivities, Black History luncheons, Honors Convocations, Commencements, Founders Day Observances, and Lyceum Series, just to list a few.

In recognition of special service, Mrs. Prater was among other honorees to receive the Distinguished Music Alumni Award from her alma mater, Hampton University, in April of 1993, during its 125th anniversary celebration. Additionally, her original musical setting of "The Candlelight Song" was set in The Links' Book of Songs at the National Conference during the summer of 1994. The Links, Inc., founded in 1946, is one of the oldest and largest volunteer service organizations of women who are committed to enriching, sustaining and ensuring the culture and economic survival of African Americans and other persons of African ancestry.

An avid volunteer, Mrs. Prater worked tirelessly with a number of community organizations including the Board of Directors of Peach County Habitat for Humanity Advisory Council, The Fort Valley Alumnae Chapter of Delta Sigma Theta Sorority, Inc., The Fort Valley Chapter of the Links, Inc., and the Board of Directors for the Girl Scouts of Middle Georgia, Inc.

Dr. Johnny Carter, retired professor of Ornamental Horticulture at FVSC's College of Agriculture, Home Economics and Allied Programs, initiated the effort to honor Mrs. Prater with a namesake daylily. Dr. Carter prepared documents to have the flower, *Jacqueline, The First Lady 1995*, registered with the American Hemerocallis (Daylily) Society.

First Lady Prater honored at Daylily ceremony
Photo courtesy FVSU Ag Marketing

Originally developed in 1994 by John Cranshaw, Daylily Hybridizer, the new hybrid was named in honor of Mrs. Prater at a ceremony held at the University Centennial Tea in the C. W. Pettigrew Farm and Community Life Center on June 11, 1995.

Dr. and Mrs. Prater are the parents of two sons, Marcus L. and Oscar L. Mrs. Jacqueline Polson Prater served faithfully as FVSU's first lady until her death in 1998.

SOURCES: Obituary; HR 1462-Prater, Jacqueline Polson condolences; Daylily Cultivar Demonstration, Agricultural Research Program, FVSU, 1995; *Notes from the Valley*, Vol. 4, No. 9, March 1998.

Dr. Oscar L. Prater
Sixth President, Fort Valley State College/
Fort Valley State University, 1990-2001
Photo courtesy FVSU Archives

I have been asked, more than once, over the past couple of months what I would like my legacy to be. I am proud of the Presidential Scholars Program, the Outstanding Faculty Award, the enormous increase in the endowment and the technological infrastructure. But perhaps more than any other endeavor, I am most proud of the bridges built and partnerships formed. Fort Valley State University has succeeded in enhancing its reputation within the University System, around the State, and across the Nation.

Oscar L. Prater

President FVSC - June 30, 2001 Retirement Celebration

Education is the greatest gift we can give our youth because it is the key that can open the door to countless opportunities. For 100 years, Fort Valley State College has provided continuous educational services to this community, state, and nation. Throughout its history, many students have entered its portals and obtained unique educational experiences, and in its role as a service institution, a host of activities and programs have made life better for the immediate community and the larger community as well.

The Flame has chronicled a century of Fort Valley State College's history and memories into its exciting pages. Many notable accomplishments have been high-lighted—accomplishments for which we are all proud. This Centennial edition burns even brighter because it records the ending and a new beginning: 'A Rich Heritage—A Bright Future.'

The 1995 Centennial class carries our appreciation for all you have accomplished here and our sincerest wishes for prosperity in your endeavors. It is our hope that your accomplishments will reflect the outstanding training that you have received here. We look forward to your successes as alumni of one of this nation's finest institutions. It has been a pleasure and a privilege to be your President and your Friend. Those of us remaining will continue to be committed to the task of carrying the torch of higher learning to even higher heights.

Congratulations and commendations to the Flame staff and advisors for a job well done.

Oscar L. Prater

President's Message, (*Flame*, 1895-1995)

In June 1990, Oscar Lewis Prater was chosen as the sixth president of the Fort Valley State College. The period of his administration would turn out to be a momentous decade in the history of the institution. Prater came to Fort Valley from Hampton University where he had been serving as vice president. A native of Alabama, Prater earned a B.A. degree in Mathematics from Talladega College, M.A. degree from Hampton University, M.S. and Ed.D., degrees from the College of William and Mary. His teaching experience included stints at Rappahannock Community College and the public schools of Williamsburg, Virginia. Among his scholarly credentials was being a contributing author to *The Status of Blacks in Higher Education* (1989). Based on the foregoing, Prater undoubtedly continued FVSC's tradition of well-qualified leadership.

President Prater's administration started with a bang—FVSC's computer science program commenced with Title III funding and immediately gained national attention and praise. In May of 1993, the School of Education, Graduate Programs and External Degrees met the new and more stringent standards of the National Council for Accreditation of Teacher Education (NCATE) and were accredited by that agency. One year later, the Board of Regents of the University System of Georgia authorized FVSC to award the Education Specialist Degree with a major in Guidance and Counseling. Also in 1994-95, the school began its centennial celebration, with enrollment exceeding 2,900 students. To highlight these years, a new computer technology and mathematics building opened, and FVSC advanced to a Level IV School by the Southern Association of Colleges and Schools (SACS).

The most significant change of the Prater Administration came in 1996 when, after several years of campaigning, the institution was granted university status by the state. The new name was the Fort Valley State University, a State and Land Grant University. This change led to new emphasis on scholarship for both faculty and students. FVSU began to gain regional and national leadership in several academic areas. The Land Grant mission also continued to advance as signified by the opening of the Meat Technology Center as part of the College of Agriculture in 1998.

In 2001, Oscar Prater, grieved by the loss of his wife Jacqueline three years before, retired as Fort Valley State University's president. He later accepted the presidency of his alma mater, Talladega College.

Historical Timeline: Dr. Oscar L. Prater, 1990-2001

1990 Dr. Oscar L. Prater appointed as the sixth President of Fort Valley State College on August 9

Athletic Field House completed

1991 Extension Communication Center (Print Shop) constructed

1994 FVSC Centennial Inauguration and Founders' Day Celebration held on November 3

1995 FVSC celebrated 100th Anniversary

Computer Technology Mathematics (CTM) Building opened on August 18

FVSC changed in status from Level III to Level IV School by Southern Association of Colleges (SACS)

Veterinary Science Laboratory Animal Facility completed and the Veterinary Technology Program was housed in new facility

Dairy Technology Laboratory added to the Georgia Small Ruminant Research and Extension Complex

1996 Fort Valley State College designated by the University System of Georgia as Fort Valley State University (FVSU), a State and Land-Grant University

Renovation of teaching laboratories in the Alva Tabor Agriculture Building completed

University convocation unveiled new University seal

Newly constructed access road named University Boulevard on October 1

1997   Meat Technology Laboratory added to the Georgia Small Ruminant Research and Extension Center

1998   FVSU commemorated "A Celebration of Fifty Years of Service in Agriculture and Home Economics as a Land Grant Institution."

Ribbon Cutting Ceremony held for opening of the Meat Technology Center, College of Agriculture, Home Economics and Allied Programs, April 21

2001   Dr. Oscar Prater retired as president of Fort Valley State University.

SOURCES: *The Flame,* 1895-1995 edition; June 30, 2001 Retirement Celebration Commemorative Booklet; and www. Fvsu.edu-history

Academic Building
Photo courtesy FVSU Archives

Aama Nahuja
Photo courtesy FVSU
Marketing

Kofi Lomotey and Aama Nahuja
Photo courtesy FVSU Marketing

Chapter 9

Aama Nahuja
Served with Dr. Kofi Lomotey, 2001-2005

"We were extremely excited by the number of participants last year. It was an outstanding event and a great way to spend Saturday morning. This year we expect an even greater turn out," said A. Nahuja.

Office of University Relations, News release, October 1, 2003 - 2nd Annual FVSU: Straight to the Top - 3K+ Fun Run/Walk October 11, 2003, hosted by marathon runner and FVSU's first lady, A. Nahuja

At the author's request, the seventh first lady of FVSU provided an interesting snapshot of her life. "Aama Nahuja, addressed as Nahuja (Nah-who- juh), is the spouse of the 7th President of Fort Valley State University, Dr. Kofi Lomotey, to whom she has been married since 1977. A native of Houston, Texas, Nahuja, with her family, resided in many cities because of her father's career as civil engineer with the federal government. Nahuja lived in Tirrenia, Italy, during elementary and junior high and graduated from Frankfurt American High School in Frankfurt, Germany. She earned a B.A. degree in government from Oberlin College in Oberlin, Ohio."

"At Oberlin, Nahuja met her soulmate, Kofi Lomotey, and they welcomed the birth of their first son, Juba. During her time there, she nurtured her passion for intellectualism, internationalism, and U. S. democracy. Upon completing her Oberlin degree, Nahuja was admitted to the Master in Library Science program at Case Western Reserve University in Cleveland, Ohio and graduated in 1979."

"When the family moved to California, Nahuja worked in the Stanford Law library before becoming a children's librarian in East Palo Alto. The family welcomed the birth of their second son, Mbeja, during this time. Nahuja later worked as a law librarian at the firm Gaston Snow & Eli Bartlett before entering the University of Santa Clara Law School in Santa Clara, California. Nahuja transferred to the State University of New York at Buffalo Law School after her first year. She obtained her J.D. in 1989. Subsequently, Nahuja obtained a federal clerkship in Buffalo under the Honorable John T. Curtin for the Western District of New York."

"In 1994, the family moved to Baton Rouge, Louisiana. Nahuja then enrolled in a Master of Law program focused on human rights at the Louisiana State University (LSU) Paul Hebert Law Center. Her thesis considered international law in two cases—the 1841 Amistad case and the 1994 Sale (Haitian interdiction) case. She also worked in the LSU Office of Academic Affairs and as coordinator of (the internal and external) program review."

"In 1997, Nahuja and Dr. Lomotey moved to Brooklyn, NY. She became a law professor at City University of New York (CUNY) Law School at Queens College in Queens, New York. She taught family law and co-taught a related law seminar for first year students. Later, Nahuja became assistant counsel at the Center for Law & Social Justice (CLSJ), a non-profit social and legal entity housed at Medgar Evers College, CUNY. CLSJ handled class action (civil rights) lawsuits, voting rights, collaborations and referrals."

"Nahuja moved to Fort Valley in 2002 after the appointment of her husband as the seventh president of Fort Valley State University; but she continued to work with CLSJ. In Fort Valley, Nahuja also pursued her interests in health and fitness by hosting the annual Straight to the Top - 3K+ Fun Run/Walk. Nahuja trained and participated in the New York City Marathon the same year."

She enjoyed working on initiatives to support FVSU students and promote the university. At the start of fall semester, President Lomotey and

Nahuja participated in the student induction ceremony and welcomed new Wildcats to FVSU. In recognition of the Sixth Annual National Education Association's (NEA) Read Across America in 2003, Peach County Library invited Nahuja as a special guest reader. To the delight of several preschoolers, she read the book *Bringing the Rain to Kapiti Plain* by Verna Aardema. At the conclusion of the session, Children's Coordinator, Nancy Rairdon, presented Nahuja a certificate and donated the book, *Noah's Ark* illustrated by Jerry Pinkney, to the library's collection in her honor.

Nahuja reads to children
at Peach County Library
Photo courtesy FVSU Marketing

Nahuja with supporters at
annual Fun Run/Walk event
Photo courtesy FVSU Marketing

Nahuja and President Lomotey travelled on many occasions to represent Fort Valley State University. For instance, they joined other representatives from HBCU's at the Thurgood Marshall Scholarship Fund's Annual Leadership Institute. FVSU students also attended the conference and networked with corporate and non-profit executives to gain information and explore today's ever-changing business world.

Nahuja's involvement also was evident in the renovation of campus apartments for special guests through generous donations provided by Lyda Hanna and Alma Bass. President Lomotey and Nahuja entertained students, faculty, staff and special guests often at the university or in the comfort of their residence.

The annual Welcome Back Reception held in January followed by the fall dinner at the Faculty and Staff Institute served as tremendous morale boosters.

The FVSU Family anticipated the backyard barbeque gatherings, a special treat indeed. Receptions hosted for renowned guest lecturers and scholars who participated at the African World Studies Institute and the Center of International Programs and Services brought excitement to the university family. Homecoming Week at Fort Valley State was always a festive occasion filled with an array of activities. Of course, walking with her husband along the parade route, ahead of colorful floats and high stepping bands while greeting employees, students, alumni and friends of the university, made it special.

The foregoing makes it clear that Nahuja juggled many activities as first lady at FVSC in addition to her roles as wife and mom.

In 2005, Dr. Lomotey resigned as president of Fort Valley State University and the family relocated to Nashville, Tennessee. Nahuja became a law librarian at the Alyne Queener Massey Law Library at Vanderbilt University.

SOURCES: Resume' 2010; The Fort Valley Statement, Vol. 2, No.1, September 2002, 1; *The Fort Valley Statement*, Vol. 2, No. 2, 3, October 2002; *The Fort Valley Statement*, Vol. 2, No. 5, March-April 2003, 3; *The Fort Valley Statement* Vol. 3, No. 2, Nov-Dec 2003, 3

Dr. Kofi Lomotey
Seventh President, Fort Valley State University, 2001-2005
Photo courtesy FVSU Marketing

Allow me to take this opportunity to say "welcome back" to all returning faculty, staff, administrators and all continuing students. I also want to welcome all new students to the Valley!

As we enter a new academic year, it is important to reflect on where we are going as an institution-as a family. Not unlike many other institutions of higher education, FVSU is in a process of change. We believe that the changes we are pursuing are for the better-better for our students, today and tomorrow; better for our faculty, staff and administrators; and better for Fort Valley and Georgia. I believe that we are a fine institution that can become a better institution. Our students of today and tomorrow deserve it. Imagine with me...

- *Imagine an institution with participatory leadership.*
- *Imagine an institution with a world-renowned African World Studies Institute.*
- *Imagine an institution where all employees are hired because they have relevant skills.*
- *Imagine an institution with several outstanding academic programs and with the remainder being at least good.*

- *Imagine an institution that routinely displays good customer service.*
- *Imagine an institution with good financial practices, as the norm.*
- *Imagine an institution where staff communicates with each other.*
- *Imagine an institution that fosters leadership skill development in its students.*

These things do not occur overnight; they may not occur in a month or a year. The point is that they can occur-at FVSU. In order for them to occur, we have to work together as a team-faculty, students, staff, administrators and alumni. We can become a better institution. Let's work together to take FVSU: Straight to the top!

Kofi Lomotey

From the President's Pen, The Fort Valley Statement, Vol.2, No. 1, University Relations, September 2002

In October 2001, Dr. Kofi Lomotey became the seventh president of The Fort Valley State University. Lomotey had an impressive academic background. He held a B. A. degree from Oberlin College in 1974, M.Ed. degree from Cleveland State University in 1978, and the M.A. (1981) and Ph.D. (1985) degrees from Stanford University. He was editor of the journal, *Urban Education,* and author or co-author of several books including, *The Racial Crisis in American Higher Education* (1991) and *Going to School: The African American Experience* (1990). He had been a faculty member at Louisiana State University and the State University of New York-Buffalo (SUNY) and came to FVSU from the position of senior vice president at Medgar Evers College–City University of New York (CUNY). He had also established a pre-school/early elementary program for African American children in Oberlin, Ohio.

Lomotey sought to make noteworthy revisions in the curriculum at FVSU, promoting the awareness of Africa and the heritage of its people. The initial step was the creation of the African World Studies Institute, a semi-autonomous unit of the institution that would be a center of research and teaching. The new emphasis was soon evident in campus activities such as the African World Film Festival that commenced in 2002.

In 2002, the Georgia General Assembly passed House Resolution 1669, introduced by Representative Calvin Smyre of the 136th District, commending Kofi Lomotey as one of the State of Georgia´s most distinguished citizens and a leading light in the state´s academic community. The resolution also recognized Lomotey's academic and scholarly accomplishments along with positive contributions to the lives of thousands of young people throughout his career.

In 2004, the Board of Regents approved a baccalaureate degree in African World Studies. Lomotey also established the John W. Davison Lecture Series, named in honor of the first principal of the Fort Valley High and Industrial School, bringing to campus such celebrities as Cornell West, Louis Henry Gates, Benjamin Carson and Michael Eric Dyson.

During Lomotey's tenure, a new satellite campus opened in Warner Robins. The campus expansion also included the opening of a new facility in downtown Fort Valley. The much anticipated completion of the Health and Physical Education facility delighted the FVSU family and community.

In 2005, President Lomotey resigned. He then moved to Fisk University as executive vice president and provost. Dr. William H. Harris was appointed interim president of FVSU.

Historical Timeline: Dr. Kofi Lomotey, 2001–2005

2001   Dr. Kofi Lomotey appointed as seventh President at Fort Valley State University on October 15.

Ribbon cutting ceremony held for the newly acquired Evans Building downtown

2002   The African World Studies Institute established

Alma Bass, FVSC Alumna, donated money to repair the historic clock tower at Founders Hall Building.

First annual African World Film Festival

Computer, Technology and Mathematics Building renamed the W. W. E. Blanchet Building after third FVSC president

Lady Wildcats captured the SIAC title for basketball for the third consecutive year.

John W. Davison Lecture Series initiated

2003   Ribbon cutting ceremony held for opening of Fort Valley State University's satellite site in Warner Robins on October 26

Fort Valley State University received approval to offer a dual degree program in Food and Nutrition/Hotel Administration.

The American Meteorological Society's (AMS) on-line Weather Studies Diversity Program: WeatherNet established

2004   Fort Valley State University received the 2004 Trumpet Award for Higher Education Institution of the Year, presented by the Trumpet Award Foundation, Inc.

Health and Physical Education Complex completed

Fort Valley State University received approval to offer degrees in Liberal Studies and African World Studies.

2005   Dr. Kofi Lomotey resigned as president.

SOURCES: www.fvsu.edu-History; Resume'

Betty H. Rivers
Photo courtesy FVSU Marketing

Larry and Betty Rivers
Photo courtesy FVSU Marketing

Chapter 10

First Lady Betty Hubbard Rivers
Served with Dr. Larry E. Rivers, 2006 – 2013

Dr. Johnny Carter, retired professor of horticulture at the Fort Valley State University, and Ann Walton, former executive director of the American Camellia Society, asked me to consider a camellia as my namesake. Of course, the idea of selecting a flower to bear my name and having it propagated for others to enjoy was music to my ears. So, in the spirit of humility and gratitude, I am honored to have a flower as my namesake, First Lady Bettyjean. Now, let's celebrate with a cup of tea.

Betty H. Rivers

2009 Calendar, Celebrating Possibilities – in Celebration of the Bettyjean Camellia

Being the first of seven children loved and nurtured by Willie James and Annie Mae Hubbard, I received my formative education in Jeffersonville, Georgia, located in Twiggs County. In 1969, I entered Fort Valley State College (now University), earning a bachelor's degree in business education four years later.

In 1973, my career began as secretary in the president's office at Florida A & M University (FAMU), Tallahassee, Florida. After two years at the university, I secured employment with the City of Tallahassee, and enrolled at Florida State University, earning a master's degree in vocational education. In 1979, Larry E. Rivers and I exchanged wedding vows in Tallahassee, Florida. Rivers and I met previously as undergraduate students at Fort Valley State College. Later, we celebrated the birth of two sons, Larry O. and Linje' E.

Additionally, I am affiliated with in Alpha Kappa Alpha Sorority, Inc., the Fort Valley State University Alumni Association, and the National Association for the Advancement of Colored People.

After thirty years of service with the City of Tallahassee, my colleagues hosted a special event in April 2006. Before a large crowd, I ended my service with the city as Business Services Manager at the Tallahassee Regional Airport. Among my primary duties, I was responsible for oversight of marketing, public relations and advertising initiatives; contract services for airport tenants and vendors; event planning and customer service initiatives. Later, I would realize that this job prepared me well for my role as first lady.

As noted previously, after graduating high school, my home away from home experience began at Fort Valley State College, until graduation in 1973. Fast-forward thirty-three years, I returned to the Valley in 2006 and started a new chapter in my life! Dr. Larry E. Rivers, my spouse, began his tenure as eighth president on March 14. In his first address to administrators, faculty, staff and students, President Rivers announced a new initiative, 'Communiversity', the engagement of FVSU and community in mutually benefiting partnerships. I embraced this idea also.

When I was introduced as First Lady Betty Rivers during spring Commencement in May before a large crowd of faculty, staff, students, parents and other visitors, the title seemed so special. I find it interesting, though, there was no clue that it would transform into endless opportunities for me to serve FVSU students and the middle Georgia community.

At the conclusion of my short, three-week retirement, I wandered over to Hunt Elementary School before the end of the school term in May. Being an avid volunteer, the school granted my request to read to third grade students. About twenty-five students along with their teacher, Mrs. Thompson, assembled in the Media Center. During the reading session, word traveled around the school that First Lady Betty Rivers had read to Mrs. Thompson's class. Well, the librarian suggested that I read to all third grade classes. By the end of the week, 75 energetic third grade students listened attentively as I read books. Again, it was a wonderful way to end my brief retirement. A few months later, I accepted the invitation to participate as a Celebrity Reader in a program sponsored by the American Association of University Women (AAUW). The group invited individuals to read at elementary schools in Warner Robins. It was a wonderful experience.

In May, I also delivered the keynote address at Twiggs County High School spring Commencement. Of course, the hometown crowd welcomed me back with open arms. The honorarium was much appreciated, and it was shared with the student who earned class Salutatorian. She entered FVSU in fall 2006.

One month later, another exciting project appeared on my radar. After contacting staff at the Boys and Girls Club of Georgia Heartlands about hosting a fieldtrip to a local museum, I prepared a proposal. Leslie Harrell, FVSU Marketing Director, assisted me by presenting the proposal to request free tours for the club at the Museum of Aviation, Robins Air Force Base. It received the stamp of approval and a new partnership was formed between the Museum of Aviation, FVSU and the Boys and Girls Club. The museum staff conducted tours for several groups of children and also shared information about military aircraft and various exhibits. Additionally, they learned about careers in aviation. At the conclusion of the in-depth tour, the museum applauded the Boys and Girls Club staff for bringing a group of children who were very eager and excited about learning what goes on in the aviation industry. They expressed appreciation for the array of questions posed by the children and their attention to detail after viewing the exhibits. The club received an invitation from the museum to visit again in the future.

This partnership has continued for several years and hundreds of children have experienced an educational, yet exciting trip to the museum, the first such trip for most. At the sixth Annual Corporate Dinner hosted by the Boys and Girls Club of Georgia Heartlands, I received a plaque inscribed with this text, *First Volunteer Service Award*, for services rendered to the Club, a great honor indeed.

Daddy's 56 Chevy Wagon
Photo courtesy FVSU Marketing

As a spin-off of this initiative, FVSU agreed to assist the Museum of Aviation at its annual car show, *Wings and Wheels*. President Rivers, an antique car collector, embraced the idea excitedly and requested that the museum assist in organizing a car, truck and bike show at FVSU. It was exciting for me since I was asked to serve on the committee along with university staff. Thus, *Wheels in the Valley, Car, Truck and Bike Show* made its debut in spring 2007. The annual show draws large crowds of car, truck and bike enthusiasts to the campus. The partnership with the Aviation Museum continues to date.

By this time, the Macon Telegraph discovered that I was on a roll and published an article about my new initiatives on July 23, *FVSU First Lady Making Her Own Mark on Campus*. From this point, with an abundance of inspiration and a clear vision for my role as first lady, the wheels began to turn rapidly.

First Lady Rivers and Mayor John Stumbo
Photo courtesy FVSU Marketing

During the first year, Fort Valley Mayor John Stumbo extended membership on the Mayor's Housing Force. I accepted it and attended the
initial meeting. To my delight, the role of the committee included assist-
ing underserved areas with housing improvements through collabora-
tion with other entities in the community. Prior to my retirement in
Tallahassee, one of my tasks included monitoring federal grants awarded
by the Department of Housing and Urban Development. Specifically,
the grant funds targeted low and moderate-income families. After learning about the Rebuilding Together Committee, another brainchild of
Mayor Stumbo, I volunteered to join that group as well since it focused
on serving local residents who needed minor home repairs. I learned
quickly that when Mayor Stumbo spoke, people responded positively. A
few years later, he requested that I serve on the Fort Valley Community
Foundation Board of Directors. I accepted the offer and considered it
a vote of confidence in my leadership skills. I also served as chair of the
foundation. Through these initiatives, I have worked with some of the
finest individuals in Fort Valley.

A new student initiative was brought to my attention a few months later. At the request of two male employees, Donald Moore and Rufus Montgomery, they suggested that I host a forum for women. After several meetings with Dr. Terrance Smith, dean of students, I began to plan a special session for female students. Dr. Smith suggested a title for the forum, Sip-N-Chat with First Lady Betty Rivers. The theme, "Catching the Dreams for tomorrow, Preparing Young Women for the 21st Century," seemed appropriate. At the inaugural event on October 12, 2006, more than 150 students attended. To date, fourteen forums have been held for students at the beginning of each semester. Again, The *Sip-N-Chat with First Lady Betty Rivers and Friends* became a much anticipated event, and the attendance increased as well. These forums promoted FVSU history, academic success, etiquette, spoken word, dress for success, healthy minds and bodies, healthy relationships, school spirit and much more.

Flyer- Sip-N-Chat with First Lady Rivers and friends
Photo courtesy FVSU Marketing

First Lady Rivers hosts residence hall forum
Photo courtesy FVSU Marketing

Since the Sip-N-Chat continued to gain popularity, the FVSU residential housing director requested forums for all campus students.
Beginning in fall 2010, residential life staff scheduled forums in the
residence halls. More than 600 dorm residents attended and listened
attentively to my talk about respecting faculty, staff and peers, support-
ing university athletic teams, and participating in extra-curricular programs and community service activities. During fall 2011, over 1,000
students attended the forum with new topics and activities including:
the FVSU History Jeopardy game, the "I am greater than AIDS" video,
spoken word, a fashion show, a special power point presentation *Know
What Men/Women Know About Relationships* and other pertinent topics.

During a meeting in fall 2006 with Gene Sheets, president, Peach
County Chamber, we discussed hosting Business after Hours to support
the chamber. President Rivers also embraced the idea. Mr. Sheets and I
began to plan the event over the next several months. During the planning process, he put forth a new idea that would result in a long-term

relationship. He asked me to serve as a member of the chamber's Board of Director's. I graciously accepted the appointment in the spirit of 'Communiversity' (Served 3 terms).

A new initiative coordinated by various local groups was a first to welcome any FVSU president. The City of Fort Valley, City Commission, Peach County Board of Commissioners, and Fort Valley Utility Commission hosted a public reception to welcome FVSU's first family at Blue Bird. There was much excitement about this event because it supported President Rivers' vision to promote 'Communiversity.'

For spiritual enrichment, I joined a Bible Study Group hosted at the First United Methodist Church in Warner Robins. Over the years, these ladies and I have bonded. They have also attended special events at FVSU. The inspirational study sessions and fellowship make my day.

United Methodist Church bible
study group, Warner Robins, GA
Photo courtesy FVSU
Marketing

During the start of the 2006 fall semester, President Rivers and I welcomed new students to FVSU. Of course, this ushered in football season.

The President's Office assisted in preparing a guest list for home games in the President's box at Wildcat Stadium. The weeklong Homecoming schedule of activities was exciting as well. I settled a bet, suited up and performed with the FVSU cheerleaders at the Homecoming Week kick-off event. Imagine that!!!

I enjoyed the annual Queen's Tea and other Homecoming festivities. By the end of the 2006 football season, President Rivers and I had attended most of the out of town games to support the Wildcats and the new coaching staff.

First Lady Rivers –
Wildcat cheerleader
Photo courtesy FVSU
Marketing

First Lady and President Rivers with Miss
Fort Valley State, Shanoria Morgan
Photo courtesy FVSU Marketing

Another speaking engagement commitment evolved for me during our first year. The FVSU Warner Robins Area Alumni Chapter requested my attendance as keynote speaker at the 3rd Annual Eugene Leverson Jr. Scholarship Banquet in November. The banquet, which is to assist FVSU students, was held in memory of the late Eugene Leverson, FVSU alumnus.

During the fall, the FVSU Family also celebrated Founders' Day, and it was delightful. The annual event recognized eighteen founders who paved the way for the establishment of the Fort Valley State University. In addition, the FVSU Family also collected donations to purchase Thanksgiving dinners for distribution in the community. President Rivers and I traveled with staff members and delivered delicious meals designated for special families in the community. The year ended with the annual Commencement exercise. It was an occasion to congratulate graduating seniors for their accomplishments and parents who supported them during college.

Thanksgiving Holiday meal delivery team
Photo courtesy FVSU Marketing

By this time, President Rivers and I had traveled to cities through-out Georgia and around the nation. We attended events hosted by FVSU alumni chapters, churches, and various professional and community based organizations. Yes, the City of Montezuma even invited the President and First Lady to serve as grand marshals in the Christmas Parade.

At year's end, it was difficult to imagine that the First Lady's schedule could be so busy. But, the first year ended on a high note.

Our second year at FVSU started out with a bang. President Rivers and I joined faculty, staff and students at the annual memorial M. L. King March. As part of the activities, local churches are selected to host the inspirational service. Since our arrival, this event has grown to several hundred participants, a marvelous sight indeed.

L-R, President Rivers, Martin
Luther King, III, Charlia
Williams, Rufus Green and
First Lady Betty Rivers
Photo courtesy FVSU Marketing

First Lady Betty Rivers and
President Rivers greet Former
Ambassador Andrew Young
Photo courtesy FVSU Marketing

After hearing many favorable comments about the annual Black History Scholarship Luncheon, I realized that it was the largest scholarship fundraiser hosted annually at the university. A group of committed individuals, including staff and community supporters, met for several months to plan this event. It regularly attracts hundreds to FVSU.

The second forum of the Sip-N-Chat with First Lady Betty Rivers and Friends delighted a large crowd of female students. Now, I realize that it really was a great idea to engage female students in empowerment forums.

A public speaking opportunity at a local church in Butler, Georgia expanded my reach in the community. Later, the pastor was invited to participate in the prayer service to kick off the president's inauguration.

Established in 2002, the John W. Davison Lecture Series has attracted famous guests who inspire, educate, entertain and empower FVSU students. Students anticipate these events and the community also. President Rivers and I hosted receptions for our guests. We have entertained actors, news anchors, rap artists, historians, actors and other notable men and women of distinction.

As mentioned previously, the Peach County Business After-Hours was initiated in 2006. The inaugural event was a tremendous success. About three hundred individuals attended the event in February 2007. Of course, Eugene Sheets and I along with FVSU staff put in many long hours to ensure its success. Now, five years later, it is recognized as the regional event of the year. Proceeds from the silent auctions at the events are split to support the chamber's operations and the new Camellia Scholarship Initiative for FVSU students that will be highlighted later.

Business After-hours at FVSU
Courtesy of FVSU Marketing

Another must attend event is the annual Ham and Egg Breakfast (established in 1916, originally named the Ham and Egg Show). Coordinated by The College of Agriculture, Family Sciences and Technology, this nationally acclaimed event attracts state legislators who provide updates about agricultural issues that impact local communities. The delicious breakfast satisfied my palate. I also engaged in great conversation with our guests.

The second year also featured the President's Inauguration. To my delight, I was asked to serve on the Inauguration Committee. My contributions included planning the kick-off prayer service and concert. I also assisted with the inauguration ceremony and reception. On March 14, 2007, President Larry E. Rivers was officially installed as Fort Valley State University's eighth president. It was indeed a labor of love and involved the work of many loyal and dedicated individuals. Comments received about the inauguration indicated it was the best ever hosted at FVSU. Yes, I was pleased that it was a great success.

At the annual Honors Convocation, students took center stage and received certificates and special awards for academic achievements. The FVSU faculty, staff and parents attended in great numbers. I enjoyed it very much, especially the opportunity to greet and chat with parents, up close and personal.

For the first time in the history of FVSU, the president, first lady, and about a dozen student performers, traveled around the state of Georgia in mid-March to recruit new students. During spring break, everyone loaded the bus in the wee hours of the morning to visit high school students and recruit new students for the fall semester. This initiative resulted in a significant spike in our enrollment. My husband and I also enjoyed bonding with FVSU students during the weeklong tour.

President and First Lady Rivers with
Wildcat Force Recruitment Team
Photo courtesy FVSU Marketing

After the university's spring break, President Rivers and I participated in the community's annual housing blitz. Coordinated by the local Rebuilding Together Team, we assisted by painting the porch of one participant who was selected to receive assistance. It was a great way to support a community initiative.

Again in 2007, I began to assist the President's Office in preparing scripts to honor Trailblazers. During spring Commencement, these persons were honored for special services rendered to the university.

First Lady Rivers escorted
during Commencement
Photo courtesy FVSU
Marketing

This trend has continued to date. On other occasions, I also prepare presidential proclamations that offer condolences to families after the passing of a FVSU graduate or for special recognition at university events. I am delighted to serve when needed.

Another highlight for the year occurred in July. President Rivers and I attended the inspirational service hosted at Blue Bird Body Company for employees. The president appeared on program and offered prayer. The keynote speaker, former president Jimmy Carter, mesmerized the audience with his words of wisdom. After the program, we enjoyed having lunch with President Carter. He sat between us and we engaged in conversation; I had one ear and the president had the other. We really enjoyed spending quality time with President Carter.

President and First Lady Rivers with
Former President Jimmy Carter
Photo courtesy FVSU Marketing

As first lady, many organizations invite me to participate in special activities. Students have been asked to accompany me also. The Macon Youth Detention Center invited the first lady to host a pep rally at their campus in 2007. The FVSU Chief of Police joined me along with several students. It was a great experience and provided the opportunity to mentor residents as well. About three years later, I accepted a second invitation to visit the center. On this occasion, the Wildcat Force, a twelve-member performance ensemble, inspired the residents by performing a remix of R&B, rap and old school favorites.

During new student 2007 fall orientation, the Orientation Committee requested that I greet students and speak on this topic: *The Importance of Learning from Mistakes.* It went well. From that point, I joined the committee and assisted with various activities to ease the transition for students from high school to college. Since 2009, the first forum for new student orientation has started with the first lady's overview of FVSU's history. On many occasions, students have assisted and developed exciting, and informative power point presentations. They also participated in original skits that I penned. Performers received great applause from the audience.

For the first two years, my schedule was booked solid with a variety of annual events such as Commencement (spring and fall), Founders Day Observance, Honors Convocation, Ham and Egg Breakfast, John W. Davison Lecture Series, Pancake Breakfast and Homecoming. At most of these events, President Rivers and I entertained guests who traveled from cities near and far. On many occasions, we received favorable comments about our beautifully, manicured campus, superb hospitality and outstanding food service. Again, I assisted university staff with the delivery of Thanksgiving meals to individuals in the community. Looking ahead, this trend continues along with other events and activities.

By now, you have probably surmised that the first lady's schedule is fast paced and very hectic. Well, you're right on that point, but there are a few more things that you should know about me as the first lady.

L-R: First Lady Mary Perdue, Governor Sonny Perdue, First Lady Betty Rivers, Dr. Charles King, Dr. Larry E. Rivers and Mrs. Patricia Rivers King
Photo courtesy FVSU Marketing

My frequent visits to Massee Lane Botanical Gardens in Marshallville, located eight miles from Fort Valley, have been soothing and relaxing. At my request, the Boys and Girls Club agreed to coordinate a field trip to the botanical gardens, a first for many. The activities included a tour of the gardens and the creation of a fabric-collage. Fine Arts Department Chair Bobby Dickey designed the collage and I cut approximately 10,000 pieces of fabric, according to his estimation, that formed the petals, blades of grass, sunbeams and squares of sky needed to complete, *The Camellia Garden*. Later, the young artists were honored at a public unveiling to celebrate their accomplishments and presented with framed certificates followed by a reception. The mural now hangs in the lobby of the Boys and Girls Club of Georgia Heartlands, a gift from me.

The Camellia Garden mural
Photo courtesy FVSU Marketing

A crowning moment for me occurred on a spring-like day in February 2009. During a ceremony on February 13, the American Camellia Society and the Fort Valley State University College of Agriculture, Home

Economics and Allied Programs unveiled a beautiful, multi-layered dark pink camellia to honor me in the presence of family, friends and FVSU supporters. The garden, *"Blossoms in the Valley: The Betty Jean Rivers Camellia Garden"* is home for the plant, "First Lady Bettyjean." Chris Daniel, Plant Operations Supervisor, designed it. Under my direction, a commemorative camellia calendar produced by staff and students along with other products generated significant funds to establish the Betty H.Rivers Camellia Scholarship Fund.

First Lady Rivers speaks at
the Camellia ceremony
Photo courtesy FVSU
Marketing

In spring of the following year, a new initiative was introduced to support the fund also. During a special ceremony, seventy-four commemorative bricks were unveiled that included the names of camellia scholarship donors. Again in 2011, the annual brick ceremony continued and featured the special unveiling of wrought iron benches.

Charlia Williams unveils
her bench in the Bettyjean
Camellia Garden
Photo courtesy
FVSU Marketing

About two months later, Fort Valley Main Street included the garden in the "Tour of Gardens." More than 150 participants stopped by to visit the garden. They were very impressed with the beautiful landscaped garden, the gazebo and sculptured fish spewing fresh water into a small basin. It made me proud. We also had the plant, First Lady Bettyjean, available for sale to customers.

Another special event took center stage to support the Camellia Scholarship Initiative mentioned earlier. The inaugural *Tea at Noon in June* with First Lady Betty Rivers was held on June 13, 2009. This popular event continues to date and draws large crowds. The FVSU Foundation has established an endowment with proceeds from the camellia initiatives. Additionally, nine students have received scholarships from this initiative along with allocations designated for the FVSU Marching Band Scholarship Fund and Fine Arts scholarships, totaling over $100,000.

Courtesy of FVSU
Marketing

Helen Rhea Stumbo,
mayor's wife and
Betty Rivers at Tea
at Noon in June
scholarship fundraiser
Photo courtesy
FVSU Marketing

In 2009, the Tubman African American Museum invited Fort Valley State University to tell its story. A committee was formed for this purpose, led by the first lady and Berry Jordan, director of the Anderson House Museum and Welcome Center. After a year-long effort, the committee created a new historical exhibit entitled, *Fort Valley State University: The Transformation of a Growing Institution since 1895* that took center stage at the museum on April 16, 2010. This exhibit started with artifacts from the time Fort Valley State emerged as an industrial school and extended to the modern era. It employed a combination of vintage and contemporary photographs, documents and historical artifacts to tell the story of the physical growth of the University campus, the development of its liberal arts curriculum, and its expanding positive impact on the community, the State of Georgia, and the nation.

As committee co-chairperson for the Tubman exhibit, my duties included collecting artifacts, writing and editing text, setting up room displays, and coordinating the ribbon cutting ceremony and reception. Since the exhibit featured the legacies of principals, presidents and first ladies who blazed trails in the Valley, it seemed appropriate to put these individuals on center stage. That's what I've done for them in this book. In gratitude to the Tubman Museum, I have served as board member since 2011. Additionally, Fort Valley State University hosted a benefit in fall 2012 to support the Tubman Museum's Educational Outreach Program and also secured memberships at the museum for all FVSU students.

The 2010 Tubman Museum Exhibition
Photo courtesy Bobby Dickey

In the fall semester of 2010, the Henry A. Hunt Memorial Library invited the first lady to participate as guest storyteller during National Young Readers' Week. The special guests included precious three and four year old children enrolled in FVSU's Child Development Center or daycare centers in the community. Members of the Central Union Missionary Baptist Church College Ministry joined me on this occasion. We had so much fun performing and engaging the children in various activities. There was great excitement when each child received a gift bag decorated with stickers and a little book inside, a gift from me. The following year, I accepted another invitation for a repeat performance. Members of the Alpha Beta Chapter of Alpha Kappa Alpha Sorority, Inc. accompanied me and everything went well. The team entertained pre-kindergarteners and a toddler/nursery class at FVSU's Child Development Center. Again, the children loved the little books tucked inside their bags adorned with colorful stickers.

Central Union Missionary
Baptist Church College Ministry
joins First Lady Rivers at
Young Readers Week event
Photo courtesy FVSU Marketing

There's one more event that made me proud as first lady. A news release issued by the FVSU Marketing Division announced that the Fort Valley State University's Joseph Adkins Players, First Lady Betty Rivers, and television film actress Karan Kendrick collaborated to produce a Broadway play at the historic Austin Theater, downtown Fort Valley, Georgia. This hit stage gospel play *Crowns*, written by Regina Taylor, premiered March 1-4, 2012. The cast featured FVSU students, employees and individuals from the community who delighted audiences and received standing ovations after each performance. Based on popular demand, Broadway returned to the Valley in 2013.

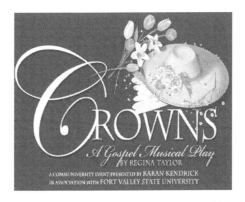

Photo courtesy Kendrick Academy and FVSU Marketing

I cannot resist including a few of the honors and commendations that have been recognitions of my tenure as FVSU's First Lady. Here are few of my favorites that I am very proud to share.

During Homecoming week of 2009, the FVSU National Alumni Association inducted three individuals into the Alumni Hall of Fame. I was one of the new inductees and honored for my accomplishments in community service. Now, you can visit the Hall of Fame Gallery in the Henry A. Hunt Memorial Library and find my portrait among others who have been honored previously.

In recognition of outstanding service to Peach County, a magazine published by the Peach Publishing Company featured, "First Ladies of Peach and Women at Work," spring 2011. I was among the ladies on the front cover, followed by an article in the magazine with additional photos.

The FVSU Foundation honored several university supporters at a surprise luncheon during Homecoming 2011, including the first lady. I received a plaque for hosting various fundraising initiatives netting more than $72,000 dollars in support of scholarships for students at FVSU. To date, the figure has risen to over $100,000.

Lastly, the Chairman's Reception hosted by Fort Valley State University alumnus, Calvin Smyre, is a highlight of the weeklong slate of events at the Fountain City Classic in Columbus Georgia. For twenty-two years, thousands of fans crowd McClung Stadium on Saturdays to watch gridiron action between the FVSU Wildcats and the Albany State University Golden Rams. Smyre honored first ladies and queens at the chairman's reception on Friday, November 4, 2011. The spotlight featured FVSU and ASU first ladies Betty H. Rivers and Jo Freeman, respectively; also Miss FVSU Kea'ya Reeves and Miss ASU Neshaszda Brown. In recognition of their contributions, the chairman showered the presidents' wives with special gifts. Congressman Sanford Bishop made a special appearance to present each with a *Certificate of Special Congressional Recognition* for outstanding achievement, service, and public distinction.

L-R: President Everett Freeman and First
Lady Jo Freeman (Albany State University),
Georgia State Representative Calvin Smyre,
First Lady Betty Rivers and Dr. Larry E. Rivers
Photo courtesy FVSU Marketing

For spiritual enrichment, President Rivers and I joined the Central Union Missionary Baptist Church after settling in Fort Valley. Rev. K. Daniel Dawsey, FVSU alum, serves as pastor. I volunteered as an advisor for the College Ministry. I could go on and on but that's probably enough shared about myself, for the moment.

L-R: Rev. K. Daniel Dawsey, First
Lady Elaine Dawsey, First Lady
Betty Rivers and Dr. Larry E. Rivers
Photo courtesy FVSU Marketing

SOURCE: FVSU Office of Marketing and Communications; Betty H. Rivers

Dr. Larry E. Rivers
Eight President, Fort Valley State University, 2006-2013
Photo courtesy FVSU Marketing

It doesn't make a difference where the Wildcats are or what they may be doing.
They may be on the gridiron, track, or field.
But, when the Wildcats hear that clarion call, they will assemble - Ta, Ta, Ta
rumble.
Yes, the Wildcats will fight, fight, and fight on.
Go Wildcats!

Larry E. Rivers

Chant, 2006

"I believe in 'Communiversity.' If you invest in the community, Fort Valley State,
the community will invest in you, and you can't do that in the confines of this
campus, Rivers said".

"I did not come to Fort Valley to do business as usual," Rivers said. "Fort Valley
students, this is a different day here. It's a new era. There are going to be changes
(so) fasten your seat belts".

Larry E. Rivers

Alumni Vision Vol. 6, No.1 spring 2006

Be Bold. Be Amazing. Be Prepared is our mantra. With the combined effort of a
dedicated leadership team, an outstanding faculty, staff, supportive community
and loyal alumni, we're developing top-notch critical thinkers who will become
leaders.

Here, amid the gently rolling hills of middle Georgia's beautiful Peach County, we
have committed to helping our students achieve their dreams.

Fort Valley State University is experiencing phenomenal growth. We have reached
milestones in a relatively short period. Student enrollment continues to soar. Our
goal was to construct new buildings equipped with the latest technology to groom
tomorrow's scientists, computer engineers and media moguls. We pushed for new

residence halls that offered students a congenial study atmosphere. Today, many of our dreams are fulfilled.

We worked hard and smart, kept our hands on the plow and our eyes fixed on achieving specific goals. For our efforts, U.S. News and World Report listed FVSU among "America's Best Black Colleges" in the #25 spot in 2011 and ranked the university #9 among the top regional public colleges in the south in its 2012 issue.

FVSU and all of its constituents will continue to build upon a 115-year tradition of success. We will reach out to every individual student to offer endless opportunities, to spur initiative and inspire real and lasting achievement.

Larry E. Rivers

FVSU website, www.fvsu.edu 2012

Dr. Larry E. Rivers returned to his alma mater as the eighth president of Fort Valley State University in February 2006. Born in the Philadelphia suburb of Sharon Hill, Rivers graduated from Fort Valley State College (now University) with a Bachelor of Science degree in social science education prior to pursuing a Master's degree in History at Villanova University in Philadelphia, Pennsylvania. Carnegie-Mellon University awarded him a Doctor of Arts degree in history and curriculum development in 1977, and Goldsmith's College of the University of London awarded him a Doctor of Philosophy degree in History in 2002.

Rivers is married to the former Betty Jean Hubbard, and they are the parents of two sons, Larry O., and Linje' E.

For more than twenty-nine years, this scholar taught history at Florida A & M University, ultimately receiving the rank of "Distinguished University Professor," one of only two on campus. Meanwhile, he also held a series of administrative appointments leading to his selection in 2002 as dean of the Florida A and M University College of Arts and Sciences.

Dr. Rivers' *Slavery in Florida, Territorial Days to Emancipation,* published in 2000, garnered three national awards. He subsequently co-authored— *Laborers in the Vineyard of the Lord: The Beginnings of the AME Church in Florida* and *For a Great and Grand Purpose: The Beginnings of the AMEZ Church in Florida*—that have received scholarly acclaim. He co-edited *Lays in Summer Lands by John Willis Menard* and *The Varieties of Women's Experiences— Portraits of Southern Women in the Post-Civil War Century.* Rivers has published a second book as sole author, *Rebels and Runaways—Slave Resistance in Nineteenth-Century Florida,* released in 2012.

Teaching, research, publishing and community service have earned the scholar numerous citations for excellence. *Ebony* magazine featured Dr. Rivers as one of America's future black leaders.

He is a member of Alpha Phi Alpha Fraternity, Inc., the Fort Valley State University National Alumni Association, Inc., the National Association for the Advancement of Colored People, Sigma Pi Phi (The Grand Boule) Fraternity and Prince Hall Masonic Lodge.

Rivers had a vision of Fort Valley State being greater than ever, and in forty-eight months, he transformed FVSU's structure. There were no longer deficits. Enrollment and morale elevated as Wildcat pride flourished. The Renaissance prompted the state's premier business publication, *Georgia Trend,* to recognize the major accomplishments made so quickly during the new president's tenure in office. In January 2008, the magazine named Rivers among the "100 Most Influential Georgians." FVSU was also listed among the "Best Places to Work in Georgia" in one of the monthly publications later that year.

In 2010, Fort Valley State's growth remained steady as Rivers began executing his plan to make his school a competitive force in higher education. The most significant changes are apparent in the areas of enrollment and the number of new construction projects completed. Student enrollment spiked to the highest level ever in the school's 115-year history. *Georgia Trend* expanded its recognition and spotlighted Dr. Rivers in its "Georgia's Top 25 Leaders" September 2010 issue. The magazine praised Dr. Rivers' outstanding leadership for the university's growth and commented on his commitment to diversify the university.

The completion of multi-million dollar construction projects and new student housing on the 1,365-acre campus made FVSU a more competitive attraction for college-bound high school, transfer and non-traditional students. In August 2010, FVSU's staff, faculty and students celebrated the addition of the newest facility, the Student Amenities Building, part of a $12 million project that included a new football stadium. The Wildcats football team proudly showed off on the gridiron when the facility opened. As of 2012, the 28,000-square-foot facility houses Chick-fil-A and Quiznos restaurants, a bookstore and a conference room. It doubles as a sports venue during home games and features several skyboxes for Wildcat fans.

Another construction project was christened in August 2010. The 63,356 square-foot Academic Classroom and Laboratory Building, with a $16 million price tag, houses laboratories, classrooms, offices and conference rooms. Prior to Rivers arrival, construction projects totaled only $30 million between 1976 and 2006. However, under Rivers' leadership from 2006 to 2012, the value of capital projects has increased to nearly $180 million. The cost to construct a new student-housing village named the Wildcat Commons is included in the figure.

Because of the tremendous expansion at the university, city officials in Fort Valley put measures in place to prepare for anticipated growth that the town of 8,600 residents will experience in upcoming years. The town's existing infrastructure will be expanded to accommodate the increasing demand for utilities and sewer services along with the revitalization of State University Drive. A $1.5 million boost came from the U. S. Department of Transportation to allow for continuation of the streetscape and beautification initiative on the main thoroughfare leading to the FVSU campus. A request for funding was submitted by the Middle Georgia Regional Commission (MGRC), under USDOT's TIGER II program and approved.

College rankings released for universities around the nation offered hope and encouragement. In previous years, FVSU was unranked by U.S. News Media group, however; for two consecutive years; the university made the list of *America's Best Black Colleges* and in 2010, the #25 spot belonged to Fort Valley State University. Its designation appeared in the 2011 edition of *America's Best Colleges* published in the September issue of *U.S. News & World Report*. FVSU is the only state-funded HBCU in Georgia ranked in the issue. Spelman College holds the number one spot.

Based on the foregoing, much progress has been made at Fort Valley State University since Dr. Rivers arrived in 2006. Although he faced budget challenges, declining enrollment, aging buildings and loss of accreditation for teachers training initially, the university also experienced a great awakening. Teacher accreditation was re-accredited, student enrollment increased significantly, several new buildings were constructed and older buildings were renovated. Lastly, the Southern Association of Colleges and Schools Commission lifted a year-old warning and reaffirmed the university's accreditation in December 2012. President Rivers often extended credit to his administrative team, FVSU Family, alums and the community for their role in making the university strong and viable.

In November 2012, Dr. Larry E. Rivers announced his intention to resign as president of the Fort Valley State University, effective June 30, 2013. University System of Georgia (USG) Chancellor Hank Huckaby named Kimberly Ballard-Washington, assistant vice chancellor for legal affairs at USG, to serve as interim president of the Fort Valley State University in June 21, 2013.

Historical Timeline: Dr. Larry E. Rivers, 2006-2013

2006

- Dr. and Mrs. Larry E. Rivers began a scholarship fundraising initiative with $100,000 donation

- Communiversity concept embraced to strengthen the university's ties with the community through service and collaborative programs

- Warner Robins Center reopened after having been closed in 2005

- Wildcat Force Student Recruitment Team initiated. President and First Lady Rivers traveled with the Wildcat Force Performing Group to high schools around the state for seven years

- *Valley Times* faculty, staff, student, and alumni newsletter initiated

- FVSU student newspaper, *The Peachite*, reinstituted

- New student residential housing complex with 951 beds commenced (Wildcat Commons, phases I and II)

- President's Trailblazers Awards for "Outstanding Service to the University and Community" introduced

- FVSU received $763,000 grant from the United States Department of Interior, along with $300,000 from the Board of Regents to initiate renovation and stabilization of historic Huntington Hall, at that time shuttered for approximately two decades

- FVSU enrollment stabilized after multi-year decline

- Fort Valley State University, City of Fort Valley and Peach County formed State University Drive Corridor Improvement Zone partnership

- Rayfield Wright Street dedicated in honor of Fort Valley State University alumnus, NFL Hall of Fame and Dallas Cowboy Legend Larry Rayfield Wright

- Fort Valley State University National Alumni Hall of Fame reactivated and relocated to Henry Alexander Hunt Memorial Library

- FVSU hosted first legislative luncheon for Georgia state representatives and lawmakers

- Centennial Monument (Wildcat Statue) erected and dedicated at Homecoming

2007

- Fort Valley State University executed agreements with Central Georgia Technical College and Middle Georgia Technical College as the first of many agreements aimed at ensuring a smooth transition for students matriculating from technical schools to the university

- FVSU cited as one of the "Best Places to Work in Georgia" by Georgia Trend magazine

- FVSU established first President's Research Mini-Grants to provide every full-time faculty member with an opportunity to enhance academic credentials toward tenure and otherwise to advance the university's scholarly mission

- FVSU established first Office of Sponsored Programs Grant Award Cost Sharing Initiative in an effort to acknowledge and reward principal investigators and the departments in which they serve for outstanding abilities to secure grants and contracts

- Larry E. Rivers received Citizen of the Year Award from the Peach County Chamber of Commerce

- Artistic representation of the Founders Hall Clock Tower installed by Fort Valley Mayor John Stumbo and dedicated at the entrance of State University Drive

- FVSU endowment recorded an increase of 20 percent over the previous fiscal year

- U.S. Department of Agriculture allocated $2.5 million for construction of new Family Development Center

- More than 300 entrepreneurs representing area Chambers of Commerce networked at FVSU for the first Business After Hours event led by First Lady Betty Rivers.

- Inaugural Wheels in the Valley: Car, Truck and Motorcycle Show held at FVSU, assisted by the Museum of Aviation, attracting hundreds of spectators

- Fall 2007 enrollment increased to 2,542 from 1,976 in 2006, with a historic high freshmen enrollment—an increase of more than 17%, the largest in the University System of Georgia

- FVSU's $5.5 million Educational and General deficits for the 2004-05 and 2005-06 academic years were eliminated with a balanced budget in 2006-07. Every year thereafter, FVSU successfully balanced its budget.

- Electronic Engineering Program received renewed Accreditation Board for Engineering and Technology, Inc. (ABET) accreditation

- Dr. Larry E. Rivers, First Lady Betty Rivers, Dr. Anne Gayles Felton, Rep. Calvin Smyre and Dr. and Mrs. Keith McRae inducted into FVSU's 1895 Pioneer Society for individual contributions of $100,000 to the university

- FVSU Cooperative Developmental Energy Program (CDEP) executed a memo of understanding with Zoo Atlanta

- $44 million Wildcat Commons (Phase I and II), a 951-bed student residential complex opened Fall 2007

- $19 million state-of-the art SMART Classroom and Laboratory Building launched, October 2007

- Newly constructed Head Start Center opened in Vienna, GA

- Dr. Larry E. Rivers, Dr. Ozias Pearson, Mr. Paul L. Thompkins and Mr. Robert William White inducted into FVSU's Alumni Hall of Fame

2008

- The Hendricks House, originally built in 1917, was restored and opened as the Agricultural Technology Conference Center

- The College of Education achieved reactivation and reaccreditation of the College of Education teacher educator program by the National Council for Accreditation of Teacher Education (NCATE)

- Five fully online programs approved by the Board of Regents: B.A. in Criminal Justice (a University System of Georgia Academic Franchise), Political Science, Psychology and Technical and Professional Writing; and M.S. in Rehabilitation Counseling and Case Management

- The Board of Regents also approved off-site programs in criminal justice (Atlanta and Forsyth), business administration, social work, computer science and computer information systems (Warner Robins)

- FVSU Concert Choir, Concert Band and Jazz Band performed at the Kennedy Center for the Performing Arts in Washington D.C.

- President Rivers named one of Georgia Trend magazine's "100 Most Influential Georgians" in January 2008

- FVSU installed the first commemorative benches and the Wall of Honor to support the university's endowment efforts

- Groundbreaking ceremony held for $16 million Wildcat Commons Housing Complex Phase III on August 1

- Fort Valley State University's fall enrollment reached another historic high with a total enrollment of 3,055 students

- President Rivers' editorial entitled, "Are Black Universities Necessary?" appeared in the Atlanta Journal-Constitution, and his commentary aired on Georgia Public Radio, a statewide broadcast aired on 17 radio stations and reached more than 200,000 weekly listeners

- FVSU purchased downtown facility, and after renovation, opened a new Fine Arts Gallery and Studio

- Through a Housing and Urban Development grant, the university purchased thirteen dilapidated houses on State University Drive and with the city's assistance, demolished them. Also working with Mayor John Stumbo and members of the City Council, the City of Fort Valley demolished an additional thirty-seven substandard/dilapidated homes for a total of fifty. This effort improved the overall aesthetics of State University Drive

2009

- FVSU earned the #21 spot among historically black colleges and universities in the 2010 edition of America's Best Colleges by U.S. News Media Group

- FVSU Concert Choir performed during Regents' Salute to Excellence in Education Gala

- The completion and grand opening of the Wildcat Commons (Phase III), a $16-million 365 bed facility

- The fall 2009 enrollment reached another historic high of 3,503

- A new $9 million Football stadium opened in August to kick off the Wildcat football season

- FVSU Camellia Garden dedicated to honor First Lady Betty Rivers and her namesake Camellia, First Lady Bettyjean. The Camellia Scholarship Fund opened with proceeds from the inaugural Tea @ Noon in June and commemorative products which included, among other items, bricks and benches. These initiatives generated over $200,000 to provide FVSU students with much needed financial assistance

- New College of Education programs initiated: Agriculture Education 6-12, Special Education General Curriculum/Early Childhood Education P-5, Middle Grades Education 4-8 and School Counselor Education

- Online bachelor's degree programs initiated in political science, psychology and English (technical English and professional writing) and off-site programs in criminal justice, business administration and an on- line criminal justice franchise

- Minority Access, a groundbreaking educational advocacy and non-profit organization dedicated to promoting diversity on college campuses and work sites nationwide, honored Dr. Larry E. Rivers as the 2009 Role Model President during its 10th annual banquet in Washington, D.C. on Sept. 13

- FVSU initiated the webcasting of animal surgeries on the university website

- Dedication of Henry Alexander and Florence Johnson Hunt Memorial Statues at Wildcat Commons

- The opening of the SAFE Center-State Animal Facility for Emergencies-initially funded with $750,000 from the state of Georgia; the facility houses large and small animals during natural and man-made disasters

- Larry E. Rivers receives Outstanding Service Award from the National Park System Advisory Board and Interior Secretary Dirk Kempthorne

---

2010

- President Larry E. Rivers, First Lady Betty Rivers, Dr. Mark Latimore and Mr. Chris Daniel unveiled 74 commemorative bricks as a fundraiser at Blossoms in the Valley - The Betty H. Rivers Camellia Garden

- FVSU featured in the spring issue of *The Camellia Journal,* "Whirlwind Trip for new International Camellia Society President"

- 2010 spring enrollment reached another historic high of 3,728 students

- Fort Valley State University worked with Peach County Commission to rename University Boulevard to Ira Hicks Boulevard, after FVSU renowned educator and administrator, Dr. Ira Hicks

- The Fort Valley State University opened an exhibition at the Tubman African-American Museum from April 16-July 3 to showcase the university's history. The five-part show—coordinated by Berry Jordan (deceased), First Lady Betty Rivers, faculty and students—highlighted FVSU's evolution from a small industrial school to a sprawling land-grant state university.

- A ribbon cutting ceremony held on August 25 signaled the official opening of the Academic Classroom and Laboratory Building

- The Student Amenities Building celebrated its official grand opening on Aug. 11. The 28,000 square foot facility houses

---

two new restaurants – Quizno's Subs and the first Chick-fil-A restaurant on a Georgia HBCU campus

- Fort Valley State University's fall enrollment skyrocketed to the largest number in the institution's 115 year history to 3,843 new students

- The Fort Valley State University National Alumni Association, Inc. inducted First Lady Betty Rivers, Asa Boynton, and Charles Robinson into its Hall of Fame

- Fort Valley State University earned the 25th spot among "Best Black Colleges" in the 2011 edition of America's Best Colleges by U.S. News Media Group

- Georgia Trend magazine, celebrating its 25th anniversary in the September issue, named Larry E. Rivers to its list of the Top 25 Leaders in Georgia

- Larry E. Rivers selected as "One of Georgia's Most Notable," by Georgia Trend magazine

- Larry E. Rivers receives "Proclamation of Honor for Outstanding Leadership," by City of Fort Valley, Georgia

- With assistance from Mayor John Stumbo and City Council members, a $1.5 million grant was obtained from the U. S. Department of Transportation to allow for continuation of the streetscape and beautification initiative on the main thoroughfare leading to the FVSU campus. A request for funding was submitted by the Middle Georgia Regional Commission, under USDOT's TIGER II program and approved.

2011

- Fort Valley State University reached its highest number of enrollees ever during the Rivers administration with a fall 2011 enrollment of 3,895 students

- Fort Valley State University celebrates 10-year reaffirmation of accreditation by Southern Association of Colleges and Schools (SACS)

- Fort Valley State University, the only 1890 land-grant institution, was selected to participate in the Agriculture and Food Research Initiative (AFRI in Georgia) Competitive Grants program at the U.S. Department of Agriculture. As a first-time recipient, the university received nearly $1 million from the USDA's National Institute of Food and Agriculture agency to research energy crops for the next five years.

- A donation of $1.5 million presented by Congressman Sanford Bishop's district director Kenneth J. Cutts on behalf of President Obama, the U.S. Department of Defense and Bishop, benefits STEM (science, technology, engineering, mathematics) students who are CDEP participants. This donation represented the highest amount awarded to CDEP in 28 years.

- This first-ever issue of the Fort Valley State University Agriculture Research Report provides a glimpse of the compelling research conducted and presented by the faculty and administrators at conferences, workshops and symposiums throughout the world.

- Master's degree program in history approved by the BOR in the Department of History, Geography, Political Science and Criminal Justice. Three concentration tracks: general history (available for public school teachers), African-American history and military history. The program offers a thesis and a non-thesis option for applicants.

- Fort Valley State University ranked #9 among the "Best Public Colleges and Universities" in the south on the 2012 Best Colleges list published by U.S. News and World Report

- FVSU ranked fifth in the University System of Georgia (behind Georgia Tech, Georgia Regents University, University of Georgia, and Georgia State) and first among regional and comprehensive universities in garnering sponsored research dollars as of June 30, 2011. These funds totaled $17.7 million in annual awards and $37 million in multi-year awards for federal, state and local contracts

- Extensive renovations of historic Huntington and Ohio halls began

2012-13

- Annual fundraising increased from $500,000 in 2006 to $1.5 million annually in 2013

- Foundation Endowment increased from $3 million in 2006 to $7.3 million in 2013

- FVSU Fiscal Management stronger with seven years of balanced budgets and unqualified audits

- To encourage faculty research and writing, Rivers researched and published two books and seven refereed articles over a seven-year period

- FVSU continues to rank fifth among the University System of Georgia's research universities, and first among regional and comprehensive universities in garnering sponsored research dollars. From 67 proposals funded in 2006 ($7.9 million in annual funding, and $21.9 million in multi-year funding to 101 proposals funded in 2013 ($18.5 million in annual funding, and $45.6 million in multi-year funding)

- FVSU received 2013 Preservation Award from The Georgia Trust for Historic Preservation for excellence in restoring historic Huntington Hall

- The Joseph Adkins Players, First Lady Betty Rivers and television/film actress Karan Kendrick produced the Broadway play "Crowns" at Fort Valley's historic Austin Theater and at FVSU's C. W. Pettigrew Farm and Community Life Center in 2013.

- Renovation of Bishop Hall Building initiated for communications majors

- Along with NCATE accreditation, the College of Education receives second accreditation by the Council for Accreditation of Counseling and Related Educational Programs (CACREP).

- Larry E. Rivers received "2013 Jillian Prescott Memorial Award," for outstanding research by the Florida Historical Society

- Larry E. Rivers received Harry T. and Harriette V. Moore Award from the Florida Historical Society, for outstanding research for book entitled Rebels and Runaways: Slave Resistance in 19th Century Florida

- Larry E. Rivers received bronze medal award for book entitled Rebels and Runaways from the State of Florida Book Award Committee

- Refinancing of Wildcat Commons Phase II, received the S&P rating of A+

- FVSU received 100% Land Grant State Match ($5.6 million)

- First East Region SIAC Football Championship in eleven years

- Graduation rates improved from 29 percent to 34 percent

- Merged several academic programs to increase efficiency in the delivery of services to students and improve faculty resource availability

- Continuing Education Program re-instituted in Warner Robins, with Addiction Counselor Certification classes, Summer Kids University, personal and professional enhancement classes, and online professional certificates from Ed2Go and Gatlin Education

- Adult Learning Initiative, including adoption of a Prior Learning Assessment policy and process

- Military Outreach Initiative, including Service Members Opportunities Colleges (SOC) membership since 2010 with acceptance of credit from military transcripts and CLEP as recommended by the American Council on Education (ACE) guide

- University established the first FVSU Research and Service Corporation to enhance academic research and global exchanges

- Fort Valley State University ranked 116 out of 160 schools by 2013 U.S. News and World Report for "Best Online Programs"

- FVSU implemented Desire2Learn Learning Management System as platform for online instruction

- Campus fiber-optic network completely replaced with state-of-the-art technology

- FVSU implemented campus-wide wireless capability

- Campus classrooms equipped with pioneering SMART technology, including smart boards

- University installs new, up-to-date, campus email system

- Fort Valley State University moves up four places from 31st to 27th among HBCUs by 2013 U.S. News and World Report

- Dr. Larry E. Rivers resigns as president of Fort Valley State University, effective June 30, 2013. University of Georgia System (UGS) Chancellor Hank Huckaby names Kimberly Ballard-Washington to serve as interim president of Fort Valley State University in June 21, 2013. Ballard-Washington serves as the assistant vice chancellor for legal affairs for the USG.

SOURCES: FVSU Marketing and Communications Office, www.fvsu.edu

Photo courtesy FVSU Marketing

Afterword

And now, *Ladies First, Please! Celebrating First Ladies, who served with principals and presidents in the Valley,* will make its debut on center stage. It feels like members of the family have assembled for a great reunion. For the first time in the history of Fort Valley State University, a single source will include biographies of First Ladies who served with their husbands during their tenure as principals and presidents in the Valley. Oftentimes, these leaders managed to run an educational institution with meager funds and resources. But, these visionaries established partnerships with well-heeled philanthropists and tapped into state and federal funds to promote Fort Valley State University as a treasure for middle Georgia and the entire nation. Strong, bold, intelligent and talented women stood by their men in the "Valley" and offered priceless support during times of struggle and success. So, a niche has been filled. This book, **Ladies First, Please!,** will offer a glimpse of first ladies, principals and presidents who left an indelible mark in the sands of time for the benefit of generations to come.

First Lady Rivers' Photo Gallery

First Lady Rivers hosts
residence hall forum
Photo courtesy FVSU Marketing

President's Trailblazers
honored at commencement
Photo courtesy FVSU Marketing

L-R: Donovan Coley,
Victoria Sturn, Lisa Scipio,
Donald McCarthy
at Tea at Noon in June
scholarship fundraiser
Photo courtesy FVSU Marketing

Alpha Beta Chapter of
Alpha Kappa Alpha Sorority,
Inc. performs at Young
Readers Week event
Photo courtesy FVSU Marketing

L-R: President and First Lady Rivers with family
at garden dedication, Dr. Willie Mae Brooks,
Dr. Deloris Brooks and Mrs. Bernice Rembert
Photo courtesy FVSU Marketing

Mildred Rocqmore and
Earnestine Johnson unveil
their bricks at the Bettyjean
Camellia Garden
Photo courtesy FVSU Marketing

Inez Bruton and Kristie
Kenney unveil their bricks at
the Bettyjean Camellia Garden
Photo courtesy FVSU
Marketing

Made in the USA
Charleston, SC
17 April 2015